Mini Delights

✻ Mini ✦
Delights

Tiny but perfect cakes, pies, desserts & sweets

This edition published by Parragon Books Ltd in 2013
LOVE FOOD is an imprint of Parragon Books Ltd

Parragon Books Ltd
Chartist House
15–17 Trim Street
Bath BA1 1HA, UK

www.parragon.com/lovefood

ISBN 978-1-4723-2434-4

Printed in China

Created and produced by Pene Parker and Rebecca Spry
Cakes: author and home economist Joanna Farrow; photographer Noel Murphy
Pies: author and home economist Sara Lewis; photographer Stephen Conroy
Desserts: author and home economist Sara Lewis; photographer William Shaw
Sweets: author and home economist Sunil Vijayakar; photographer Karen Thomas

Notes for the Reader

This book uses both metric and imperial measurements. Follow the same units of measurement
throughout; do not mix metric and imperial. All spoon measurements are level: teaspoons are
assumed to be 5 ml, and tablespoons are assumed to be 15 ml. Unless otherwise stated, milk is
assumed to be full fat, eggs and individual vegetables are medium, and pepper is freshly ground
black pepper. Unless otherwise stated, all root vegetables should be washed and peeled prior
to using.

The times given are an approximate guide only. Preparation times differ according to the
techniques used by different people and the cooking times may also vary from those given.
Optional ingredients, variations or serving suggestions have not been included in the time
calculations.

Recipes using raw or very lightly cooked eggs should be avoided by infants, the elderly, pregnant
women, convalescents and anyone suffering from an illness. Pregnant and breastfeeding women
are advised to avoid eating peanuts and peanut products. Sufferers from nut allergies should be
aware that some of the ready-made ingredients used in the recipes in this book may contain nuts.
Always check the packaging before use.

Front cover recipe: Chocolate and amaretto truffles (page 210).

Contents

Introduction

Tiny portions of our favourite treats are fun to make and so easy to eat. They look cute and, because they are only bite-sized, they make the perfect finish for a special dinner, an informal gathering or a celebration party. The cakes include everything from delicious fruit loaves to miniature wedding cakes. Bite-sized pies made with delicious buttery pastry will melt in your mouth and are surprisingly easy to make. Impress your friends at your next dinner party by serving two or three different mini desserts on one plate for a sophisticated touch, or round off your meal with a selection of home-made sweets that look terrific and won't leave you feeling guilty.

Ingredients

Eggs

Eggs are a basic ingredient in baking. They serve many functions, providing structure, colour, texture, flavour and moisture. It is important to use organic or free-range eggs if possible. Always check the dates on the carton and use eggs that are as fresh as possible. Do not use egg substitutes in place of fresh eggs and always store your eggs in a cool place, but not in the fridge.

Flour

Plain flour and self-raising flour are both used in this book. Plain flour (also known as all-purpose flour) has a medium gluten content. It can be white or wholemeal and does not contain a raising agent. Self-raising flour can be white, brown or wholemeal, with baking powder added. It is used where a cake, biscuit or bread needs to rise. Don't substitute wholemeal flour in these recipes as it is heavier and dense and will change the texture of the recipe..

Chocolate

Plain, milk and white chocolate and cocoa powder are used in the recipes in this book. There are many brands and varieties of chocolate, and it is always worth buying the best you can afford. Plain chocolate contains at least 35 per cent cocoa solids, and can contain over 70 per cent. The higher the percentage of cocoa solids, the richer the flavour. Milk chocolate usually contains at least 25 per cent cocoa solids, and tends to consist of cocoa, butter, milk, sugar and flavourings. White chocolate is made from cocoa butter, sugar, milk solids, flavourings such as vanilla and emulsifiers such as lecithin. For advice on melting chocolate, see page 169.

Butter

The recipes specify either salted or unsalted butter. This enables you to control the amount of salt in the recipe. Do not replace butter with margarine or butter substitutes, as this will affect the texture and flavour.

Sugar and spice

The spices and flavourings used in the recipes in this book include ground ginger, ground cardamom seeds, chilli powder, vanilla extract, peppermint extract and strawberry and raspberry flavourings. Always use what the recipe specifies as substituting one for another will affect the results.

Sugars add colour, flavour, sweetness and moisture. The recipes in this book use muscovado, granulated and caster sugar, soft brown sugar, icing sugar and syrups such as golden syrup and glucose syrup. Always try to have these in your storecupboard at home as substituting one for another will affect the results.

Equipment

Cupcake & muffin cases

Mini cupcake and muffin paper cases vary considerably in size. The recipes in this book require paper cases with a base diameter of 3 cm/1¼ inches and 4 cm/1½ inches. Mini silicone cases are also available in a variety of colours. They're dishwasherproof and reusable, and cakes are easy to remove from them by peeling away the cases. To bake, simply set silicone cases on a baking tray rather than in a muffin tray or cupcake tray. Neither silicone cases nor paper cases need greasing.

Muffin tins

Paper cupcake cases and muffin cases must sit comfortably in the tin's sections, which should offer support but not crease the paper cases up. Mini cupcake tins and mini muffin tins have 12 or 24 sections; if using a 12-section tin you will need to bake two batches of cakes for some of the recipes in this book.

Sectional Muffin tins

Round and square sectioned cake tins measure 5 cm/2 inches in diameter per section and are usually bought in packs of 16, which fit onto a base for baking. Alternatively bake a large sponge cake and let it firm up for 24 hours, then cut out 5-cm/2-inch rounds or squares using a metal cutter as a guide.

Cookie cutters

Cookie cutters can be used to cut out shapes. Cutters are available in a variety of shapes and sizes and are sometimes sold seasonally, so it's worth collecting your favourite shapes when you see them. If you don't have the right size for the recipe, check your glasses, cups and saucers and cut around these. You can make pie lids from flower, heart or circle shapes stamped out with cookie cutters.

Moulds for mini desserts

You may have some dishes already, perhaps liqueur glasses, a mini muffin tin, ovenproof ramekin dishes or demitasse coffee cups. Additional dishes can be bought from specialist cook shops, the chinaware section of a department store, or online. Small plastic shot glasses can be bought in packs from supermarkets and (unlike glass) are suitable for freezing.

The dishes used are between 50 ml/2 fl oz and 150 ml/5 fl oz . Where small silicone muffin trays are used, a measurement has been given for the base of the muffin cups; metal mini muffin trays with 12- or 24-section cups are also used for some recipes. The liqueur glasses used hold 50 ml/2 fl oz.

Mini Cakes

Baking techniques

Preparing tins

Use greaseproof paper or baking paper to line tins and melted butter or vegetable oil to grease them.

Lining square tins

Place the tin on baking paper, draw around the tin and cut out the paper just inside the lines. Cut a strip the depth of the tin and make a 1-cm/½-inch fold along one long edge. Grease the tin using a pastry brush and fit the strip around the sides so the folded strip sits on the base. Snip the folded edge at the corners. Press the paper square into the base and grease the paper.

Lining round sectioned tins

Grease the sections. Cut out circles of baking paper 1 cm/½ inch larger than the section diameters. Make 5 mm/¼ inch cuts at the sides of the circles and press them in sections so the snipped edges go up the sides.

Mixing muffins

Muffins are made by adding the wet ingredients to the dry ingredients. The flour is usually sifted first. Add the wet ingredients all in one go and fold everything together gently. As soon as they're combined but with specks of flour still visible, spoon the mixture into the cases. Over-mixing muffins can make them less light.

Filling cases

Unless otherwise stated, fill cupcake cases until they're almost full and the mixture is level with the top of the cases. For muffins the mixture can extend above the tops of the cases slightly to achieve the 'muffin top'.

How to tell if a cake is cooked

Cakes are usually slightly domed in the centre with a lightly browned surface. Gently touch the surface with your flattened fingers; it should feel just firm. Some cakes require a further test of pushing a skewer into the centre; if cooked the skewer will come out clean.

Decorating techniques

Applying frostings and creams

Take a little of the frosting from the bowl using a small palette knife. Spread the frosting gently over each cake to cover it in an even layer before refining the application with the flat edge of the knife to level the surface.

Colouring ready-to-roll icing and marzipan

Using a cocktail stick, dot a little food colouring onto the icing paste. If you want a delicate colour, use a tiny amount as a little goes a long way. Working on a surface dusted with icing sugar, knead in the colour.

Covering cakes with ready-to-roll icing

Take the required amount of icing and roll it out thinly on a surface that is lightly dusted with icing sugar to between 3 mm/⅛ inch and 5 mm/¼ inch thick and 7 cm/2¾ inches in diameter. Lift over the cake and use your fingers to ease the icing around the sides, pinching it together where there's a point. Cut off the excess at these points and tuck the icing around the base before trimming off excess with a sharp knife.

Making a paper piping bag

Cut out a 25-cm/10-inch square from baking paper and fold it diagonally in half to make a triangle. Cut the paper in half, to one side of the folded line, to make two triangles. Holding one triangle with the long edge away from you, curl the right point over to meet the central point, forming a cone. Curl the left point over the cone. Adjust the points so there's no hole at the tip. Fold the points over to secure the cone in place.

Piping bags and nozzles

Piping bags can be fitted with nozzles or snipped at the tip. Half-fill the bag with icing and twist the open end together to seal. Snip off the tip and test the thickness of the piping, snipping off more if necessary. (If using a piping nozzle, cut 1.5 cm/½ inch off the tip of the bag and fit with a nozzle before filling and sealing.) The nozzles used in this book are: a large star nozzle for lavish swirls; a small star nozzle for small stars or shells; and a writer nozzle for lines and dots.

Vanilla sponge cake

Makes 1 x 18-cm/7-inch round or
 1 x 15-cm/6-inch
 square cake

Prep: 15 minutes

Cook: 40 minutes

150 g/5½ oz lightly salted
butter, softened

150 g/5½ oz caster sugar

1 tsp vanilla extract

3 eggs, beaten

175 g/6 oz self-raising flour

2 tbsp milk

When using this moist, buttery sponge cake mixture, follow the baking directions in your chosen recipe. To bake it as a sponge cake, put it in an 18-cm/ 7-inch round or square greased and lined cake tin and bake for 40 minutes, or until firm to the touch.

1. Put the butter and sugar in a mixing bowl and beat them together with an electric handheld whisk until pale and fluffy. Beat in the vanilla. Add the eggs, a little at a time, beating between each addition. (If they are added too quickly, the mixture will separate and the cake won't be as light.)

2. Sift in the flour, then stir it in gently with a metal spoon. As soon as the ingredients are combined, gently stir in the milk. The mixture should drop easily from the spoon when tapped on the side of the bowl. (For a shortcut 'all in one' method, put all the ingredients in the bowl together and beat until soft and creamy.) Cook as per your recipe or turn the mixture out into a greased and lined 18-cm/7-inch round or 1 x 15-cm/6-inch square cake tin and bake in an oven preheated to 180°C/350°F/Gas Mark 4 for 40 minutes.

Variations

White chocolate:	Replace half the sugar with 200 g/7 oz melted white chocolate, stirring it into the mixture after the eggs.
Lemon:	Add the finely grated rind of 2 lemons when creaming the butter and sugar and use 2 tablespoons of lemon juice instead of vanilla and milk.
Orange:	Add the finely grated rind of 1 orange when creaming the butter and sugar and use 2 tablespoons of orange juice instead of vanilla and milk.
Almond:	Replace 55 g/2 oz flour with 55 g/2 oz ground almonds and add 1 teaspoon of almond extract instead of the vanilla.

Buttercream

Makes: 1 quantity of
 buttercream

Put 100 g/3½ oz unsalted butter in a mixing bowl and beat with an electric handheld whisk until softened. Add 150 g/5½ oz icing sugar and beat, using the whisk, until smooth and creamy. Pour in 1 tablespoon of hot water and beat again until very soft and fluffy. For vanilla buttercream beat in 1 teaspoon of vanilla extract with the icing sugar. For lemon buttercream beat in the finely grated rind of 1 lemon with the icing sugar and use 2 tablespoons of lemon juice instead of the water.

Carrot cakes

Makes: 20
Prep: 1 hour, plus cooling
Cook: 35 minutes

Carrot cake is such an all-time favourite, it quite simply had to be included here. If you're making these in advance, the little marzipan carrots can be positioned after frosting the cake, but don't add the leafy tops more than a few hours before serving as they are likely to wilt.

150 g/5½ oz lightly salted butter, softened, plus extra for greasing

150 g/5½ oz light muscovado sugar

3 eggs

150 g/5½ oz self-raising flour

½ tsp baking powder

½ tsp ground mixed spice

85 g/3 oz ground almonds

finely grated rind of 1 lemon

150 g/5½ oz carrots, grated

85 g/3 oz sultanas, roughly chopped

DECORATION

150 g/5½ oz cream cheese

40 g/1½ oz unsalted butter, softened

115 g/4 oz icing sugar, plus extra for dusting

2 tbsp lemon juice

60 g/2¼ oz marzipan

orange food colouring

several sprigs of dill

1. Preheat the oven to 180°C/350°F/Gas Mark 4. Grease and line the base and sides of a 26-cm x 22-cm/10-inch x 8-inch roasting tin or similar sized tin. Grease the baking paper. Put the butter, light muscovado sugar, eggs, flour, baking powder, mixed spice, almonds and lemon rind in a mixing bowl and beat together with an electric handheld whisk until smooth and creamy. Stir in the carrots and sultanas.

2. Turn the mixture out into the tin and level the surface. Bake in the preheated oven for 35 minutes, or until risen and just firm to the touch. Leave in the tin for 10 minutes, then transfer to a wire rack to cool.

3. For the decoration, beat together the cream cheese, butter, icing sugar and lemon juice until creamy. Colour the marzipan deep orange (see page 10). Roll it into a sausage shape on a surface lightly dusted with icing sugar, then divide it into 20 pieces and form each one into a small carrot shape, marking shallow grooves around each with a knife.

4. Using a palette knife, spread the frosting over the cake, taking it almost to the edges. Trim the crusts from the cake to neaten it, then cut it into 20 squares. Place a marzipan carrot on each cake and add a small sprig of dill.

Cherry and almond loaves

Makes: 12
Prep: 15 minutes, plus cooling
Cook: 20 minutes

A bite-sized mini treat for those who like traditional cakes. If you don't have a silicone loaf tray, use individual metal tins — they're slightly larger and you'll have enough mixture for about 8 cakes, which will need an extra 5 minutes' cooking time.

85 g/3 oz lightly salted butter, softened, plus extra for greasing

70 g/2½ oz caster sugar

1 egg

1 egg yolk

70 g/2½ oz self-raising flour

½ tsp almond extract

55 g/2 oz ground almonds

55 g/2 oz natural glacé cherries, roughly chopped

2 tbsp flaked almonds

55 g/2 oz icing sugar

2 tsp lemon juice

1. Preheat the oven to 180°C/350°F/Gas Mark 4. Place a 12-section silicone mini loaf tray on a baking tray, or grease and base-line individual mini loaf tins. Put the butter, caster sugar, egg, egg yolk, flour, almond extract and ground almonds in a mixing bowl and beat together with an electric hand-held whisk until smooth and creamy. Stir in the cherries.

2. Using a teaspoon, spoon the mixture into the tray sections and level with the back of the spoon. Break up the flaked almonds slightly by squeezing them in your hands and scatter them over the cake mixture. Bake in the preheated oven for 20 minutes (25 minutes if using tins), or until risen and just firm to the touch. Leave in the tray for 5 minutes, then transfer to a wire rack to cool.

3. Beat the icing sugar and lemon juice together in a small bowl and drizzle over the cakes with a teaspoon. Leave to set.

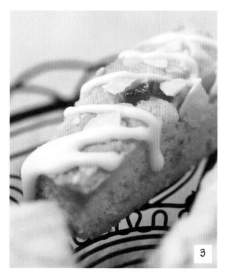

Mango cakes

Makes: 12
Prep: 15 minutes, plus cooling,
plus 2–3 hours soaking
Cook: 20 minutes

70 g/2½ oz dried mango, finely
chopped

finely grated rind of 1 orange,
plus 3 tbsp juice

25 g/1 oz creamed coconut

85 g/3 oz lightly salted butter,
softened, plus extra for greasing

70 g/2½ oz caster sugar

1 egg

85 g/3 oz self-raising flour

icing sugar, for dusting

Dried mango and creamed coconut give these little tea cakes a fresh, tropical flavour, heightened by a subtle hint of orange. Moist and buttery, they'll keep in an airtight container for several days.

1. Preheat the oven to 180°C/350°F/Gas Mark 4. Place a 12-section silicone mini loaf tray on a baking tray, or grease and base-line individual mini loaf tins. Put the mango and orange juice in a small bowl and leave to stand, covered, for 2–3 hours, or until the orange juice is mostly absorbed. Finely grate the coconut (if it's very firm and difficult to grate, warm it briefly in the microwave first).

2. Put the coconut, butter, sugar, egg, flour and orange rind in a mixing bowl and beat together with an electric handheld whisk until smooth and pale. Stir in the mango and any unabsorbed orange juice.

3. Using a teaspoon, spoon the mixture into the tray sections and level with the back of the spoon. Bake in the preheated oven for 20 minutes (25 minutes if using tins), or until risen and just firm to the touch. Leave in the tray for 5 minutes, then transfer to a wire rack to cool.

4. Serve lightly dusted with icing sugar.

Mini Victoria sandwich cakes

Makes: 12
Prep: 20 minutes, plus cooling
Cook: 15 minutes

70 g/2½ oz lightly salted butter,
softened, plus extra for greasing

70 g/2½ oz caster sugar

70 g/2½ oz self-raising flour

1 egg

1 egg yolk

1 tsp vanilla extract

DECORATION

150 ml/5 fl oz double cream

6 tbsp strawberry jam

85 g/3 oz icing sugar

1 tbsp lemon juice

So tiny and dainty, these 'doll's house'-sized sponges are just right with a cup of tea when you don't want anything too rich or filling. Because of their size they'll dry out quickly, so store them in an airtight container or freeze if making ahead.

1. Preheat the oven to 180°C/350°F/Gas Mark 4. Place a 12-section silicone mini muffin tray on a baking tray, or grease and base-line a 12-section mini muffin tin. Put the butter, caster sugar, flour, egg, egg yolk and vanilla in a mixing bowl and beat together with an electric handheld whisk until it is smooth and creamy.

2. Using a teaspoon, spoon the mixture into the tray sections and level with the back of the spoon. Bake in the preheated oven for 15 minutes, or until risen and just firm to the touch. Leave in the tray for 5 minutes, then transfer to a wire rack to cool.

3. For the decoration, whip the cream until it just peaks. Split the cakes in half horizontally using a small serrated knife. Press 2 tablespoons of the jam through a small sieve into a bowl to extract the seeds. Put the sieved jam in a small paper piping bag and snip off the tip (see page 10). Sandwich the cakes together with the remaining jam and cream.

4. Beat the icing sugar and lemon juice together in a bowl until smooth. Spoon the icing over the cakes, spreading it just to the edges. Pipe dots of jam on top of each cake and draw a wooden skewer through them.

Iced baby bundt cakes

Makes: 12
Prep: 20 minutes, plus cooling
Cook: 15–20 minutes

This bundt recipe is made with cinnamon, walnuts and apples for a really moist texture. Don't be put off if you don't have mini bundt tins; any small tins with a similar capacity can be used just as effectively.

200 g/7 oz plain flour, plus extra for sprinkling

1 tsp baking powder

1 tsp ground cinnamon, plus extra for sprinkling

125 g/4½ oz caster sugar

60 g/2¼ oz walnuts, finely chopped

2 small dessert apples, peeled, cored and finely grated

6 tbsp vegetable oil, plus extra for greasing

3 eggs

150 ml/5 fl oz buttermilk

ICING

3 tbsp natural yogurt

150 g/5½ oz icing sugar, sifted

1. Preheat the oven to 180°C/350°F/Gas Mark 4. Brush 2 x 75-ml/2½-fl oz mini bundt tins with vegetable oil. Sprinkle a little flour into the tins and tilt so that both the bases and sides are coated; tap out the excess.

2. Sift the flour, baking powder and cinnamon into a mixing bowl. Stir in the caster sugar, walnuts and apples.

3. In a separate mixing bowl, beat together the oil, eggs and buttermilk. Add them to the dry ingredients and mix to form a soft paste.

4. Using a teaspoon, spoon the mixture into the tins and level with the back of the spoon. Bake in the preheated oven for 15–20 minutes, or until risen and just firm to the touch. Leave in the tins for 5 minutes, then transfer to a wire rack to cool.

5. For the icing, put the yogurt into a bowl and add the icing sugar. Beat together well until smooth. Spoon a little of the icing onto the top of each cake, easing it slightly down the sides with the back of the spoon so the icing runs down the flutes around the sides. Lightly sprinkle the tops of the cakes with cinnamon.

Coffee crumb cakes

Makes: 18
Prep: 30 minutes, plus cooling
Cook: 30–35 minutes

55 g/2 oz lightly salted butter, softened, plus extra for greasing

100 g/3½ oz caster sugar

1 egg

5 tbsp soured cream

125 g/4½ oz self-raising flour

TOPPING

85 g/3 oz plain flour

70 g/2½ oz lightly salted butter, cut into pieces

½ tsp ground mixed spice

1½ tsp ground espresso coffee

70 g/2½ oz caster sugar

ICING

85 g/3 oz icing sugar

1 tbsp strong espresso coffee

One of these treats is an ideal accompaniment to a mid-morning cup of tea or coffee. The crumb topping is sweet and streusel-like, in delicious contrast to the light and airy sponge underneath it.

1. Preheat the oven to 180°C/350°F/Gas Mark 4. Grease and line the base and sides of an 18-cm/7-inch shallow, loose-bottomed square cake tin. Grease the baking paper.

2. For the topping, put the plain flour, butter, mixed spice and coffee in a food processor and blend until the mixture starts to resemble coarse breadcrumbs. Add the caster sugar and blend again briefly. Tip the mixture into a mixing bowl.

3. For the sponge, put the butter, caster sugar, egg, soured cream and self-raising flour in the food processor and blend until smooth and creamy, then turn out into the tin and level the surface. Sprinkle the crumb mixture in an even layer on top. Bake in the preheated oven for 30–35 minutes, or until risen and just firm to the touch and a skewer inserted into the centre comes out clean. Leave in the tin for 10 minutes, then transfer to a wire rack to cool.

4. For the icing, put all but 2 tablespoons of the icing sugar in a small mixing bowl and add the coffee. Beat to a smooth paste that falls in a thick trail from the spoon, adding a little more icing sugar if necessary. Cut the cake into 3 even-sized pieces, then cut across to make 18 rectangular pieces. Drizzle with the icing.

gooey chocolate fudge bites

Makes: 21
Prep: 25 minutes, plus cooling
Cook: 35 minutes

200 g/7 oz lightly salted butter, cut into pieces, plus extra for greasing

200 g/7 oz plain chocolate, roughly chopped

100 ml/3½ fl oz double cream

3 eggs

150 g/5½ oz light muscovado sugar

100 g/3½ oz self-raising flour

ICING

200 g/7 oz plain chocolate

3 tbsp golden syrup

55 g/2 oz unsalted butter, cut into pieces

70 g/2½ oz icing sugar, sifted

This is as rich and delicious as chocolate cake can be! It's moist and gooey, with a generous amount of chocolate fudge icing. Store in a cool place rather than in the fridge so that the texture doesn't spoil.

1. Preheat the oven to 160°C/325°F/Gas Mark 3. Grease and line the base and sides of a 20-cm/8-inch square cake tin. Grease the baking paper.

2. Put the butter, chocolate and cream in a heatproof bowl, set the bowl over a saucepan of gently simmering water and heat until melted. Leave to cool slightly.

3. Put the eggs and light muscovado sugar in a mixing bowl and beat together with an electric handheld whisk until the mixture begins to turn frothy. Stir in the cooled chocolate mixture. Sift in the flour and stir it in gently.

4. Turn the mixure into the tin and level the surface. Bake in the preheated oven for 35 minutes, or until risen and just firm to the touch. Leave in the tin for 10 minutes, then transfer to a wire rack to cool.

5. For the icing, put 175 g/6 oz of the chocolate in a small heavy-bottomed saucepan with the syrup and butter. Heat gently, stirring frequently, until the mixture is smooth and glossy. Transfer the mixture to a mixing bowl and beat in the icing sugar. Leave until the icing has thickened enough to just hold its shape.

6. Split the cake in half horizontally and spread half the fudge icing on the cut side of the bottom piece. Place the other piece on top, cut-side down, and spread the remaining icing on top of the cake. Using a sharp knife, carefully cut thin shards from the remaining chocolate. (If it's too brittle, heat very briefly in the microwave and try again.) Trim off the edges of the cake to neaten it, then cut it into 21 rectangles. Scatter the shards on top.

Chocolate brownies

Makes: 25
Prep: 15 minutes, plus cooling
Cook: 18–20 minutes

These little brownies have the familiar sugary crust and soft gooey centre that we've come to know and love. They're impossible to resist, so it's a good thing they're only bite-sized!

115 g/4 oz lightly salted butter, cut into pieces, plus extra for greasing

100 g/3½ oz plain chocolate, roughly chopped

2 eggs

175 g/6 oz light muscovado sugar

2 tsp vanilla extract

55 g/2 oz plain flour

25 g/1 oz cocoa powder

40 g/1½ oz pecan or walnuts, roughly chopped

1. Preheat the oven to 200°C/400°F/Gas Mark 6. Grease and line the base and sides of an 18-cm/7-inch shallow, loose-bottomed square cake tin.

2. Put the butter and chocolate in a heatproof bowl, set the bowl over a saucepan of gently simmering water and heat until melted. Leave the mixture to cool slightly.

3. Put the eggs, sugar and vanilla in a mixing bowl and beat together with an electric handheld whisk until the mixture begins to turn frothy. Stir in the chocolate mixture until combined.

4 Sift the flour and cocoa powder into the bowl and scatter in the nuts. Stir together gently, then turn the mixture into the tin and level the surface.

5. Bake in the preheated oven for 18–20 minutes, or until the crust feels dry but gives a little when gently pressed. (If you're unsure, it's better to slightly under-cook brownies as they lose their gooeyness when they are over-baked.) Leave in the tin for 10 minutes, then transfer to a wire rack to cool. Cut the cake into 25 squares.

3

4

5

Vanilla swirled brownies

Makes: 12
Prep: 20 minutes, plus cooling
Cook: 12–15 minutes

85 g/3 oz lightly salted butter, plus extra for greasing

100 g/3½ oz plain chocolate, roughly chopped

1 egg

1 egg yolk

100 g/3½ oz light muscovado sugar

40 g/1½ oz self-raising flour

¼ tsp baking powder

85 g/3 oz milk chocolate, roughly chopped

FROSTING

150 g/5½ oz mascarpone cheese

4 tbsp icing sugar

1 tsp vanilla extract

milk or plain chocolate curls, to sprinkle

These rich, chocolatey morsels are great as a teatime treat – and even better with coffee after a special dinner with friends.

1. Preheat the oven to 190°C/375°F/Gas Mark 5. Grease and base-line a 12-section mini muffin tin.

2. Put the butter and plain chocolate in a heatproof bowl, set the bowl over a saucepan of gently simmering water and heat until melted. Leave the mixture to cool slightly.

3. Put the egg, egg yolk and light muscovado sugar in a mixing bowl and beat together with an electric handheld whisk until the mixture begins to turn frothy. Stir in the melted chocolate. Sift the flour and baking powder into the bowl, scatter in the milk chocolate and stir together. Using a tea-spoon, spoon the mixture into the tray sections.

4. Bake in the preheated oven for 12–15 minutes, or until the crust feels dry but gives a little when gently pressed. (If you're unsure, it's better to slightly under-cook brownies as they lose their gooeyness when over-baked.) Leave in the tray for 10 minutes, then transfer to a wire rack to cool.

5. For the frosting, put the mascarpone cheese, icing sugar and vanilla in a small bowl and beat with an electric handheld whisk until smooth and creamy. Put the mixture in a piping bag fitted with a 1-cm/½-inch star nozzle and pipe swirls over the cakes. Sprinkle with chocolate curls.

Blueberry and vanilla muffins

Makes: 18
Prep: 10 minutes, plus cooling
Cook: 15 minutes

125 g/4½ oz self-raising flour

½ tsp baking powder

70 g/2½ oz caster sugar

85 g/3 oz blueberries

2 tsp vanilla extract

1 egg

125 ml/4 fl oz buttermilk

2 tbsp vegetable oil

vanilla sugar, for dusting

In these fresh blueberry muffins, the plump, juicy fruits burst during baking to colour and flavour the light, airy sponge. This recipe uses homemade paper cases, made by pressing squares of baking paper into the muffin tray.

1. Preheat the oven to 190°C/375°F/Gas Mark 5. Cut out 18 x 9-cm/3½-inch squares from baking paper. Push the squares into 2 x 12-section mini muffin tins, creasing the squares to fit so that they form paper cases. Don't worry if they lift out of the sections slightly; the weight of the muffin mixture will hold them in place.

2. Sift the flour and baking powder into a mixing bowl. Stir in the sugar and blueberries. In a separate mixing bowl, beat together the vanilla, egg, buttermilk and oil with a fork until evenly combined.

3. Tip the buttermilk mixture into the flour. Using a dessertspoon, gently fold the ingredients together until only just mixed. (Don't over-blend the ingredients or the muffins won't be as light.)

4. Spoon the mixture into the paper cases; it should be level with the top of the tin. Sprinkle with a little vanilla sugar and bake in the preheated oven for 15 minutes, or until risen and just firm to the touch. Leave the muffins in the tin for 2 minutes, then transfer them in their cases to a wire rack to cool. Serve warm or cold, dusted with extra vanilla sugar.

1

2

4

Cranberry muffins

Makes: 18
Prep: 10 minutes, plus cooling
Cook: 12–15 minutes

These muffins can be prepared and baked in less than half an hour, perfect for a relaxed weekend breakfast. For flavour variations, try adding the grated rind of an orange or a sprinkling of ground ginger or cinnamon.

100 g/3½ oz self-raising flour

½ tsp baking powder

55 g/2 oz caster sugar

100 g/3½ oz dried cranberries, roughly chopped

100 ml/3½ fl oz natural yogurt

1 egg

2 tbsp vegetable oil

icing sugar, for dusting

1. Preheat the oven to 190°C/375°F/Gas Mark 5. Line 2 x 12-section mini muffin tins with 18 x 3-cm/1¼-inch mini paper cases.

2. Sift the flour and baking powder into a mixing bowl. Stir in the caster sugar and cranberries. In a separate mixing bowl, beat together the yogurt, egg and vegetable oil with a fork until evenly combined.

3. Tip the yogurt mixture into the flour. Using a dessertspoon, gently fold the ingredients together until only just mixed. (Don't over-blend the ingredients or the muffins won't be as light.)

4. Spoon the mixture into the paper cases; it should be level with the top of the tin. Bake in the preheated oven for 12–15 minutes, or until risen and just firm to the touch. Leave the muffins in the tin for 2 minutes, then transfer them in their cases to a wire rack to cool. Serve warm or cold, dusted with icing sugar.

2

3

4

Double chocolate muffins

Makes: 12
Prep: 15 minutes, plus cooling
Cook: 15 minutes

Because these muffins are tiny, it's only right that they're as packed with chocolate as they could be! Any that are not eaten fresh from the oven can be kept for two days in an airtight container. Warm them for a few minutes in a moderate oven to revive their flavour.

15 g/½ oz cocoa powder

70 g/2½ oz self-raising flour

¼ tsp baking powder

25 g/1 oz light muscovado sugar

85 g/3 oz milk chocolate, roughly chopped

1 egg

3 tbsp milk

40 g/1½ oz lightly salted butter, melted

40 g/1½ oz plain chocolate, roughly chopped

1. Preheat the oven to 190°C/375°F/Gas Mark 5. Line a 12-section mini muffin tin with 3-cm/1¼-inch mini paper cases.

2. Sift the cocoa powder, flour and baking powder into a mixing bowl. Stir in the light muscovado sugar and milk chocolate. In a separate mixing bowl, beat together the egg, milk and butter with a fork until they are evenly combined.

3. Tip the egg mixture into the flour. Using a dessertspoon, gently fold the ingredients together until only just mixed. (Don't over-blend the ingredients or the muffins won't be as light.)

4. Spoon the mixture into the paper cases; it should be level with the top of the tin. Bake in the preheated oven for 15 minutes, or until risen and just firm to the touch. Leave the muffins in the tin for 2 minutes, then transfer them in their cases to a wire rack to cool.

5. Put the plain chocolate in a heatproof bowl, set over a saucepan of gently simmering water and heat until melted. Using a teaspoon, drizzle the melted chocolate over the muffins and serve warm or cold.

Maple and banana cupcakes

Makes: 12
Prep: 20 minutes, plus cooling
Cook: 18–20 minutes

1 small banana

2 tbsp maple syrup

2 tbsp milk

60 g/2¼ oz lightly salted butter, softened

70 g/2½ oz caster sugar

1 egg, beaten

100 g/3½ oz self-raising flour

FROSTING

150 g/5½ oz lightly salted butter, softened

1 tsp vanilla extract

6 tbsp icing sugar

7 tbsp maple syrup

8 pecan or walnut halves, roughly chopped, to decorate

Banana cake invariably appeals to everyone, from tiny tots to adults. These mini ones can be served plain, simply dusted with icing sugar, or swirled with the delicious maple butter frosting.

1. Preheat the oven to 180°C/350°F/Gas Mark 4. Line a 12-section mini muffin tin with 3-cm/1¼-inch mini paper cases.

2. In a small mixing bowl, mash the banana to a purée with a fork. Stir in the maple syrup and milk.

3. Put the butter and caster sugar in a separate mixing bowl and beat together with an electric handheld whisk until light and fluffy. Gradually beat in the egg, a little at a time, adding a teaspoon of the flour if the mixture starts to separate.

4. Sift half the flour into the bowl containing the butter mixture, then add half the banana. Gently fold the ingredients together until only just mixed. Sift in the remaining flour, add the remaining banana mixture and fold in.

5. Spoon the mixture into the paper cases. Bake in the preheated oven for 18–20 minutes, or until risen and just firm to the touch. Leave in the tin for 5 minutes, then transfer to a wire rack to cool.

6. For the frosting, put the butter, vanilla, icing sugar and maple syrup in a bowl and beat with an electric handheld whisk until smooth and creamy. Put the frosting in a small paper piping bag fitted with a 1-cm/ ½-inch star nozzle and use to decorate the cupcakes. Scatter with the nuts.

Baby shower cupcakes

Makes: 18
Prep: 45 minutes, plus cooling
Cook: 15 minutes

70 g/2½ oz lightly salted butter, softened

70 g/2½ oz caster sugar

1 egg

1 egg yolk

70 g/2½ oz self-raising flour

1 tsp vanilla extract

DECORATION

1 quantity Buttercream (see page 9)

pink and blue food colourings

55 g/2 oz ready-to-roll icing

icing sugar, for dusting

These are so simple to make, but very pretty – and perfect for the next baby shower. Pink and blue look effective together, but you can change the colour scheme to any other combination.

1. Preheat the oven to 180°C/350°F/Gas Mark 4. Line 2 x 12-section mini muffin tins with 18 x 3-cm/1¼-inch mini paper cases, preferably in deep pink or blue.

2. Put the butter, caster sugar, egg, egg yolk, flour and vanilla in a mixing bowl and beat together with an electric handheld whisk until smooth and creamy. Spoon the mixture into the paper cases. Bake in the preheated oven for 15 minutes, or until risen and just firm to the touch. Leave in the tin for 5 minutes, then transfer to a wire rack to cool.

3. For the decoration, divide the buttercream equally between 2 bowls and colour 1 with pink colouring and the other with blue, so they're pale pastel. Using a palette knife, spread a thin layer of pink icing over half the cakes and blue over the other half, reserving some for decoration.

4. Colour the remaining buttercream in the bowls to a deeper tone and put it in small paper piping bags fitted with 1-cm/½-inch star nozzles. Pipe pink shells around the blue cakes and blue shells around the pink ones.

5. Colour half the ready-to-roll icing blue (see page 10) and wrap it tightly in clingfilm. Colour the remainder pink and roll it out thinly on a surface lightly dusted with icing sugar.

6. Cut the pink icing into 1-cm/½-inch wide strips, then cut across these at 2.5-cm/1-inch intervals to make tiny rectangles. Use 2 rectangles to shape bow ends, pinching the ends together as you position them on the blue-edged cakes. Bend 2 more rectangles into loops, pinching the ends together, and secure with a damp paintbrush to complete each bow. Use the blue icing in the same way to make bows for the pink-edged cakes.

Chocolate and raspberry cupcakes

Makes: 20
Prep: 50 minutes, plus cooling
Cook: 12–15 minutes

70 g/2½ oz raspberries

55 g/2 oz cocoa powder

100 ml/3½ fl oz boiling water

55 g/2 oz lightly salted butter, softened

125 g/4½ oz light muscovado sugar

1 egg, beaten

100 g/3½ oz self-raising flour

DECORATION

40 g/1½ oz lightly salted butter

100 g/3½ oz plain chocolate, roughly chopped

2 tbsp golden syrup

40 g/1½ oz raspberries

85 g/3 oz icing sugar, sifted

Here's your chance to get carried away with special messages on these pretty cakes – hearts, kisses, whatever you fancy! Once decorated they'll keep fresh for a couple of days in a cool place.

1. Preheat the oven to 180°C/350°F/Gas Mark 4. Line 2 x 12-section mini muffin tins with 20 x 3-cm/1¼-inch mini paper cases, preferably in deep pink or brown.

2. Put the raspberries in a small mixing bowl and crush with a fork until they are broken up. In a separate mixing bowl, whisk the cocoa powder with the boiling water. Leave to cool.

3. Put the butter and light muscovado sugar in a third mixing bowl and beat together with an electric handheld whisk until light and fluffy. Beat in the egg a little at a time.

4. Stir in the flour and the cocoa mixture until evenly combined, then add the raspberries and mix together lightly. Spoon the mixture into the paper cases. Bake in the preheated oven for 12–15 minutes, or until risen and just firm to the touch. Leave in the tins for 5 minutes, then transfer to a wire rack to cool.

5. For the decoration, melt the butter in a small saucepan and add the chocolate and syrup. Heat very gently until the chocolate has almost melted, then tip into a mixing bowl. Leave to cool, stirring frequently, until the mixture has thickened enough to almost hold its shape. Spoon it over the cakes and spread to the edges using a palette knife.

6. Crush the raspberries and press them through a sieve, using the back of a spoon to extract the juice. Sift the icing sugar over the juice and stir to make a loose paste. Put the icing in a small paper piping bag and snip off the tip (see page 10). Pipe hearts and kisses onto the cakes.

Red velvet heart cupcakes

Makes: 12

Prep: 1–1½ hours, plus cooling

Cook: 15 minutes

1 small raw beetroot, about 70 g/2½ oz, finely grated

1 egg

2 tbsp buttermilk or soured cream

1 tsp vinegar

55 g/2 oz lightly salted butter, softened

25 g/1 oz light muscovado sugar

55 g/2 oz self-raising flour

2 tsp cocoa powder

DECORATION

½ quantity Buttercream (see page 11)

70 g/2½ oz ready-to-roll icing

deep red food colouring

icing sugar, for dusting

These cakes take a little while to decorate, but the results are gorgeous. Make yourself comfortable and enjoy!

1. Preheat the oven to 180°C/350°F/Gas Mark 4. Line a 12-section mini muffin tin with 4-cm/1½-inch mini paper cases, in deep red or white.

2. Put the beetroot, egg, buttermilk and vinegar in a mixing bowl and stir together until well combined. Put the butter and light muscovado sugar in a separate mixing bowl and beat together with an electric handheld whisk until pale and fluffy. Sift half the flour and cocoa powder into the butter mixture and tip in the beetroot mixture. Stir gently until evenly combined. Sift in the remaining flour and cocoa and stir again to mix.

3. Spoon the mixture into the paper cases. Bake in the preheated oven for 15 minutes, or until risen and just firm to the touch. Leave in the tin for 5 minutes, then transfer to a wire rack to cool.

4. For the decoration, spread the buttercream over the cakes using a palette knife. Colour the ready-to-roll icing deep red (see page 10).

5. Roll a 5 g/⅛ oz piece of icing into a thin rope 12 cm/4½ inches long. On a surface lightly dusted with icing sugar, flatten it with a rolling pin, keeping it no more than 1-cm/½-inch wide. Cut it in half lengthways, then across into 2.5-cm/1-inch pieces. Roll each little piece up between your thumb and finger to resemble a tiny rose. Use the roses to build heart shapes on top of all the cakes by pressing them gently down into the buttercream.

Summer flower cakes

Makes: 16
Prep: 2½ hours, plus cooling
Cook: 25 minutes

a little lightly salted butter, for greasing

1 quantity Lemon Sponge mixture (see page 11)

1 quantity Lemon Buttercream (see page 9)

900 g/2 lb white ready-to-roll icing

pink and purple food colourings

icing sugar, for dusting

These little cakes are a labour of love, but look simply stunning. If you've planned a colour scheme for a special party, you can alter the colours of the vertical stripes to enhance your theme. Once decorated, they'll keep in a cool place for several days.

1. Preheat the oven to 180°C/350°F/Gas Mark 4. Grease and base-line a cake tin containing 16 x 5-cm/2-inch sections.

2. Put a dessertspoon of the sponge mixture into each tin section. (If you have digital scales, make sure you put exactly the same amount in each section. To do this, put the prepared tin on the scales and set them to zero, then spoon 35 g/1¼ oz mixture into a section, reset the scales to zero, and fill the remaining sections, resetting the scales each time.) Bake in the preheated oven for 25 minutes, or until risen and just firm to the touch. Leave in the tin for 5 minutes before carefully loosening each cake by running a slender knife around the sides of each section. Transfer the cakes to a wire rack to cool before peeling away the base paper.

3. Reserve 3 tablespoons of the buttercream and use the remainder to spread a thin layer over the tops and sides of the cakes.

4. Reserve 300 g/10½ oz of the ready-to-roll icing. From the remainder, colour 200 g/7 oz pale pink, 200 g/7 oz purple and 200 g/7 oz a darker pink (see page 10). Take half of each coloured icing and roll it out thinly on a surface lightly dusted with icing sugar. Cut a strip from each colour that is the depth of the cakes. Cut this into 5-mm/¼-inch wide strips the depth of the cake and secure them, in alternating colours, around the sides of the cakes, pressing them gently into the buttercream. Use the remaining coloured icings to cover all the cakes.

5. Roll out the reserved white ready-to-roll icing as thinly as possible on a surface lightly dusted with icing sugar and cut out simple flower shapes using a 15-mm/½-inch plunger cutter. Press each cut flower shape out onto your finger and then place it on top of a cake. Repeat until you've built up a cluster of flowers on one cake, then repeat for all the cakes.

6. Colour the reserved buttercream pink. Put it in a small paper piping bag and snip off the tip (see page 10). Pipe little dots in the centres of all the white flowers.

White party stars

Makes: 9–10
Prep: 1–1 ½ hours, plus cooling
Cook: 25–30 minutes

unsalted butter, for greasing

1 quantity Orange Sponge
mixture (see page 11)

1 quantity Orange Buttercream
(see page 11)

400 g/14 oz white ready-to-roll
icing

1 egg white

200 g/7 oz icing sugar, sifted,
plus extra for dusting

lilac food colouring

These pretty little stars would make a great addition to a special occasion; you could substitute the colour of your choice to tie in with your party theme.

1. Preheat the oven to 180°C/350°F/Gas Mark 4. Grease and line the base and sides of a 26-cm x 22-cm/10½-inch x 8½-inch roasting tin or similar sized tin.

2. Turn the sponge mixture into the tin and level the surface. Bake in the preheated oven for 25–30 minutes, or until risen and just firm to the touch. Leave in the tin for 10 minutes, then transfer to a wire rack to cool.

3. If the cake has risen in the centre, cut off a thin slice with a large knife. Using an 8-cm/3-inch star cutter as a guide, cut out shapes from the sponge. (Cut each star shape as close to the previously cut star as possible so you don't waste any sponge; freeze the sponge trimmings for making trifle or cake pops another time.) Turn the cakes over so that the base forms a flat top.

4. Using a palette knife, spread a thin layer of buttercream over the top and sides of each star.

5. Roll out 40 g/1½ oz ready-to-roll icing on a surface lightly dusted with icing sugar to a circle roughly 11 cm/4½ inches in diameter. Lift it over a star cake and fit the sides, pinching the icing together at the points. Cut off the excess at the points and then cut around the base of the cake. Repeat with the remaining cakes.

6. Beat the egg white in a clean bowl with the half the icing sugar until smooth. Gradually work in the remaining icing sugar until softly peaking. Add a little lilac food colouring and put the icing in a small paper piping bag fitted with a little writer nozzle (see page 10). Pipe tiny dots in the centre of the tops of the cakes.

Birthday balloons

Makes: 24

Prep: 1–1½ hours, plus cooling

Cook: 18–20 minutes

1 quantity White Chocolate
Sponge mixture (see page 11)

2 quantities Buttercream
(see page 11)

350 g/12 oz chewy sweets in
3 flavours, e.g. blackcurrant,
strawberry and orange

24 x 6-cm/2½-inch lolly sticks

100 g/3½ oz small red, green and
yellow candy-coated
chocolate sweets

Kids will love these fun, colourful cakes, lavishly decorated with tempting treats. Use candles to replace some of the balloons if you prefer.

1. Preheat the oven to 180°C/350°F/Gas Mark 4. Line 2 x 12-section mini muffin tins with 4-cm/1½-inch mini paper cases, preferably in pink, green or yellow.

2. Spoon the cake mixture into the paper cases. Bake in the preheated oven for 18–20 minutes, until risen and just firm to the touch. Leave in the tin for 5 minutes, then transfer to a wire rack to cool.

3. Using a palette knife, spread a thin layer of buttercream over the cakes.

4. For each balloon, take 8 g/⅙ oz chewy sweets (about 2 sweets) and mould them into a ball. (If they are brittle or too firm to shape, microwave them on medium power for 5–6 seconds to soften them first. Don't overheat them or they'll turn to a molten syrup.) Push each balloon shape onto the end of a lolly stick. Pinch the sweet around the stick to create the effect of a knotted end. Repeat until you have enough balloons, pushing each into a cake.

5. For the streamers, soften the remaining chewy sweets as above and roll them out thinly. Cut them into 5-cm/2-inch x 5-mm/¼-inch pieces and curl each one around a lolly stick. Twist the sweets off the sticks. Scatter the cakes with the candy-coated sweets and the sweet twists to finish.

Mini party cakes

Makes: 16
Prep: 1¼ hours, plus cooling
Cook: 40 minutes

A platter of these delicious cakes will look impressive at any special get-together. Make them a couple of days in advance, so you've got time to enjoy the decorating before more pressing party tasks arise. For a big birthday use number sparklers too.

a little lightly salted butter, for greasing

1 quantity Vanilla Sponge mixture (see page 11)

1 quantity Vanilla Buttercream (see page 11)

heart-shaped sugar sprinkles

pearl balls

1. Preheat the oven to 180°C/350°F/Gas Mark 4. Grease and line the base and sides of an 18-cm/7-inch square cake tin.

2. Spoon the cake mixture into the tin and level the surface with the back of the spoon. Bake in the preheated oven for 40 minutes, or until risen and just firm to the touch. Leave in the tin for 10 minutes, then transfer to a wire rack to cool.

3. Cut a 1-cm/½-inch crust off the edges of the cake, then cut the cake into 16 even-sized squares.

4. Put the buttercream in a paper piping bag fitted with a small star nozzle (see page 10). Place the cakes in paper cake cases.

5. Pipe vertical lines down the sides and over the top edges of the cakes. Scatter the tops of the cakes with sugar sprinkles and pearl balls.

Halloween cakes

Makes: 18
Prep: 1½ hours, plus cooling
Cook: 40 minutes

a little lightly salted butter, for greasing

2 quantities Orange Sponge mixture (see page 11)

2 tbsp lemon juice

2 tbsp orange juice

3 tbsp runny honey

6 tbsp apricot jam

2 tbsp hot water

orange food colouring

750 g/1 lb 10 oz white ready-to-roll icing

icing sugar, for dusting

55 g/2 oz plain chocolate, roughly chopped

several soft green jellies

20 small Oreo cookies, filling removed

Serve these cakes at a Halloween party, or box them up for impressive 'take home' gifts. They look particularly stunning on a dark plate or cloth.

1. Preheat the oven to 180°C/350°F/Gas Mark 4. Grease and line the base and sides of a 26-cm x 22-cm/10½-inch x 8½-inch roasting tin or similar sized tin. Grease the baking paper.

2. Turn the cake mixture into the tin and level the surface. Bake in the preheated oven for 40 minutes, or until risen and just firm to the touch. Leave in the tin for 10 minutes, then transfer to a wire rack to cool.

3. If the cake has risen in the centre, cut off a thin slice with a large knife. Using a 6-cm/2½-inch half-moon cutter as a guide, cut out shapes from the sponge. Turn the cakes over so that the base forms a flat top.

4. Mix the juices with the honey in a small jug and drizzle over the surface of the cakes so the syrup seeps into the sponge. Press the jam through a small sieve into a bowl and stir in the hot water. Brush this mixture over the tops and sides of the cakes.

5. Knead orange food colouring into the ready-to-roll icing (see page 10). Roll out 40 g/1½ oz of the icing on a surface lightly dusted with icing sugar to an oval 15 cm x 10 cm/6 inches x 4 inches. Lift it over a half-moon cake and fit it around the sides, pinching the icing together at the points. Cut off the excess at these points and then cut around the base of the cake. Repeat with the remaining cakes, reserving the icing trimmings.

6. Put the chocolate in a heatproof bowl, set the bowl over a saucepan of gently simmering water and heat until melted. Put the chocolate in a small paper piping bag and snip off the tip (see page 10). Colour the icing trimmings a deeper orange and shape them into small balls. Mark 'pumpkin' ridges with the back of a knife. Cut small pieces of soft jelly and push them into the tops for stalks, securing with chocolate.

7. To shape bats, heat an Oreo cookie in the microwave until it's soft (this will take 1½–2 minutes, but check after a minute). Cut a circle from one side with a 2.5-cm/1-inch cutter. Cut small flutes from the opposite sides with a 1.5-cm/½-inch cutter. Secure the decorations in place with chocolate and pipe bat eyes and extra bats around the sides of the cakes.

Party presents

Makes: 16

Prep: 1½ hours, plus cooling
and decorating

Cook: 45 minutes

a little lightly salted butter, for greasing

1 quantity White Chocolate or Almond Sponge mixture (see page 11)

1 quantity Buttercream (see page 11)

8 tbsp apricot jam

2 tbsp brandy, almond or orange liqueur or water

850 g/1 lb 14 oz white marzipan

yellow, blue and pink food colourings

icing sugar, for dusting

55 g/2 oz white chocolate, roughly chopped

3 metres/10 feet deep pink ribbon, about 1-cm/½-inch wide

3 metres/10 feet yellow ribbon, about 5-mm/¼-inch wide

Marzipan makes a great cake covering, particularly for those who find the sweetness of icing too much. It can be coloured, rolled, cut out and shaped just as you would ready-to-roll icing, and is equally fun to work with.

1. Preheat the oven to 180°C/350°F/Gas Mark 4. Grease and line the base and sides of an 18-cm/7-inch square cake tin. Turn the cake mixture out into the tin and level the surface. Bake in the preheated oven for 45 minutes, or until risen and just firm to the touch. Leave in the tin for 10 minutes, then transfer to a wire rack to cool.

2. If the cake has risen in the centre, cut off a thin slice with a large knife so that the surface of the cake is level. Split the cake in half horizontally and sandwich the halves together with the buttercream. Cut a 5-mm/¼-inch crust off the sides. Turn the cake over and check that it's completely level. Cut the cake into 16 even-sized squares.

3. Press the jam through a small sieve into a little saucepan and stir in the brandy. Heat gently until smooth. Colour 25 g/1 oz of the marzipan yellow (see page 10) and another 25 g/1 oz blue and reserve both, wrapped separately in clingfilm. Colour the remaining marzipan pink. Brush the apricot glaze all over the tops and sides of the cake squares.

4. Roll out 55 g/2 oz of the pink marzipan thinly on a surface lightly dusted with icing sugar, to a 12-cm/4½-inch square. Lift it over a cake and fit it down the sides, pinching the excess together at the corners. Cut off the excess at these corners and then cut around the base of the cake. Repeat with the remaining cakes, reserving the marzipan trimmings.

5. Colour the marzipan trimmings a deeper shade of pink and use, with the other coloured marzipans, to shape parcels. Arrange on the cakes.

6. Put the chocolate in a heatproof bowl, set the bowl over a saucepan of gently simmering water and heat until melted. Put the melted chocolate in a small paper piping bag and snip off the tip (see page 10). Pipe lines over the parcels and around the top edges of the cakes. Cut the pink ribbon into 19-cm/7½-inch lengths and secure around the bases of the cakes with dots of chocolate from the piping bag. Cut the yellow ribbon into the same sized lengths and position these so they sit in the centre of the pink ribbon, again secured with dots of the chocolate.

Mini ivory wedding cakes

Makes: 16
Prep: 1½ hours, plus cooling
Cook: 1 hour

Make these pretty cakes for a girls' night before the big day, or of course for the wedding party itself. Bake the sponges a day before decorating so they've time to firm up a bit. Assemble the cakes a day before the party.

a little lightly salted butter, for greasing

2 quantities White Chocolate Sponge mixture (see page 11)

250 g/9 oz white ready-to-roll icing

brown or ivory food colouring

icing sugar, for dusting

16 x 7.5-cm/3-inch round silver cake cards

300 ml/10 fl oz double cream

300 g/10½ oz white chocolate, roughly chopped

10 metres (33 feet) wired organza ribbon, about
2.5 cm/1 inch wide

1. Preheat the oven to 180°C/350°F/Gas Mark 4. Grease and line the base and sides of a 23-cm/9-inch square cake tin.

2. Spoon two-thirds of the cake mixture into the tin and level the surface with the back of the spoon. Bake in the preheated oven for 35 minutes, or until well risen and just firm to the touch. Leave in the tin for 10 minutes, then transfer to a wire rack to cool. Wash and reline the tin and bake the remaining mixture for 20–25 minutes, as before.

3. Colour the ready-to-roll icing with a dash of brown food colouring (see page 10). Roll out half the icing as thinly as possible on a surface lightly dusted with icing sugar. Cut out 8 rounds using a 7.5-cm/3-inch cookie cutter, re-rolling the trimmings to make sufficient. Repeat with the other half. Dampen the surfaces of the cake cards and position a circle of icing on each.

4. To make a ganache, heat half the cream in a small saucepan until very hot but not boiling. Pour it into a mixing bowl and add the chocolate. Leave to stand, stirring frequently, until the chocolate has melted. Leave to cool completely. Stir in the remaining cream and beat lightly with an electric handheld whisk on a slow speed until the ganache is just thick enough to hold its shape. (If over-whisked it might start to separate.)

5. Using a 5-cm/2-inch round cookie cutter as a guide, cut out 16 rounds from the deeper sponge cake. Use a 3-cm/1½-inch round cutter as a guide to cut out 16 rounds from the shallower sponge. (Freeze the trimmings for making trifle or cake pops another time.) Place the larger cakes on the iced cards, securing with a little ganache. Spread some of the remaining ganache over the tops and sides of these cakes with a palette knife. Position the smaller cakes on top and cover these with ganache in the same way. Leave to set in a cool place for 1–2 hours.

6. Cut the ribbon into 60-cm/24-inch lengths and wrap a length around each cake, securing at the tops with bows and cutting off any long ends.

Mini cake pops

Makes: 24
Prep: 1–1¼ hours, plus setting
Cook: 40 minutes

450 g/1 lb cooked Vanilla or
Almond Sponge (see page 11)
or shop-bought

85 g/3 oz mascarpone cheese

70 g/2½ oz icing sugar

½ tsp vanilla or almond
extract

DECORATION

225 g/8 oz milk chocolate,
roughly chopped

24 lolly sticks

150 g/5½ oz fondant icing
sugar

pink food colouring

4 tsp cold water

24 small candy-coated
chocolate sweets

sugar sprinkles

These mini 'cupcake' cake pops have both child and adult appeal, so they're ideal for a gathering of mixed ages. Once iced, they'll keep in a cool place for a couple of days.

1. Line a baking tray with baking paper. Crumble the sponge cake into a mixing bowl. Add the mascarpone, icing sugar and vanilla and mix together until you have a thick paste.

2. Roll a 25 g/1 oz piece of the paste into a ball. Push this ball into a mini paper case, pressing it down so that when it is removed from the case you have a mini cupcake shape. Shape the remaining 23 cake pops in the same way. Place on the baking tray and chill for 1–2 hours to firm up.

3. Put the chocolate in a heatproof bowl, set the bowl over a saucepan of gently simmering water and heat until melted. Remove from the heat. Push a lolly stick into each cake pop. Dip a cake pop into the chocolate, turning it until coated. Lift it from the bowl, letting the excess drip back into the bowl, then place it in a cup or tumbler. Repeat with the remaining cake pops. Chill or leave in a cool place until the chocolate has set.

4. Put the fondant icing sugar in a mixing bowl and beat in a dash of pink food colouring and the water until smooth. The icing should almost hold its shape. Spoon a little onto a cake pop, easing it slightly down the sides with the side of a teaspoon. If the icing is too firm you might need to add a dash more water. Before the icing sets, place a small sweet in the centre of each cake pop and scatter with sugar sprinkles.

Chocolate mint cake pops

Makes: 26–28
Prep: 1 hour, plus setting
Cook: 5 minutes

300 g/10½ oz plain chocolate, roughly chopped

25 g/1 oz unsalted butter, softened

50 g/1¾ oz hard-boiled mint sweets

450 g/1 lb milk chocolate

50 g/1¾ oz mini marshmallows, roughly chopped

26–28 lolly sticks

chocolate sprinkles, to decorate

This is a cake pop version of 'rocky road', and is about as easy to make as it gets! The milk chocolate coating has family appeal, but you can use plain chocolate instead for a more adult flavour.

1. Line a baking tray with baking paper. Put the plain chocolate in a heatproof bowl, set the bowl over a saucepan of gently simmering water and heat until melted. Stir in the butter. Leave until the mixture is cool but not beginning to set.

2. Put the mint sweets in a polythene bag and tap firmly with a rolling pin until they are broken into tiny pieces. Finely chop 150 g/5½ oz of the milk chocolate, then stir it into the melted plain chocolate with the mints and marshmallows until thoroughly mixed.

3. As soon as the mixture is firm enough to hold its shape, roll 20 g/¾ oz of it into a ball. Shape the remaining cake pops in the same way. Place them on the baking tray and chill for 30–60 minutes, until firm but not brittle. Push a lolly stick into each cake pop, then chill for 10 minutes.

4. Roughly chop the remaining milk chocolate and melt as above, then remove from the heat. Dip a cake pop into the chocolate, turning it until coated. Lift it from the bowl, letting the excess drip back into the bowl, and place it in a cup or tumbler. Sprinkle with chocolate sprinkles. Repeat with the remaining cake pops. Chill or leave in a cool place until the chocolate has set.

Double chocolate whoopie pies

Makes: 12–14
Prep: 25 minutes, plus cooling
Cook: 10 minutes

70 g/2½ oz lightly salted
butter, softened

125 g/4½ oz light muscovado
sugar

1 egg

1 tsp vanilla extract

125 g/4½ oz plain flour

½ tsp bicarbonate of soda

40 g/1½ oz cocoa powder

150 ml/5 fl oz buttermilk

FILLING

200 g/7 oz milk chocolate,
roughly chopped

140 g/5 oz unsalted butter,
softened

85 g/3 oz icing sugar

70 g/2½ oz plain chocolate,
roughly chopped

chocolate sprinkles, optional

Quench your chocolate craving with these moist and morish homemade whoopies; they're so good they'll be gone before you know it!

1. Preheat the oven to 200°C/400°F/Gas Mark 6. Line 2 baking trays with baking paper. Put the lightly salted butter, light muscovado sugar, egg and vanilla in a mixing bowl and beat together with an electric handheld whisk until the mixture is thickened and pale.

2. Sift the flour, bicarbonate of soda and cocoa into a separate mixing bowl. Add half of this mixture and half the buttermilk to the butter mixture. Stir with a spatula or large metal spoon. Once combined, add the remaining flour mixture and buttermilk and carefully stir again.

3. Put the mixture into a large piping bag fitted with a 1-cm/½-inch plain nozzle (see page 10). Pipe small blobs onto the baking trays, slicing off the peaks with a small knife and spacing the blobs about 5 cm/2 inches apart to allow for expansion.

4. Bake in the preheated oven for 10 minutes, or until risen and just firm to the touch, switching over the baking trays halfway through cooking. Leave on the trays for 5 minutes, then transfer to a wire rack to cool.

5. For the filling, put the milk chocolate in a heatproof bowl, set the bowl over a saucepan of gently simmering water and heat until melted. Leave to cool slightly. Put the unsalted butter and icing sugar in a mixing bowl and beat with an electric handheld whisk until light and fluffy. Stir the melted chocolate into the butter mixture until evenly combined.

6. Sandwich the whoopie pies together in pairs with the filling. Melt the plain chocolate as above, then drizzle a little of it over each whoopie pie. Scatter with the sprinkles, if using. Leave in a cool place to firm up for a couple of hours.

Gingerbread and vanilla whoopie pies

Makes: 14
Prep: 25 minutes, plus cooling
Cook: 10 minutes

1 egg

70 g/2½ oz light muscovado sugar

1 tbsp black treacle

40 g/1½ oz lightly salted butter, melted

5 tbsp milk

150 g/5 oz plain flour

½ tsp bicarbonate of soda

1½ tsp ground ginger

½ tsp ground mixed spice

FILLING

100 g/3½ oz cream cheese

15 g/½ oz unsalted butter, softened

1 tsp vanilla extract

55 g/2 oz icing sugar, plus extra for dusting

1 tsp boiling water

These whoopies have a distinctive gingerbread flavour, perfect for autumnal comfort eating!

1. Preheat the oven to 180°C/350°F/Gas Mark 4. Line 2 baking trays with baking paper. Put the egg, light muscovado sugar and treacle in a mixing bowl and beat together with an electric handheld whisk until thickened and foamy. Beat in the lightly salted butter and milk.

2. Sift the flour, bicarbonate of soda, ginger and mixed spice into the bowl and stir with a wooden spoon to make a soft paste.

3. Spoon teaspoons of the mixture onto the baking trays, flattening them slightly so each spoonful is about 3 cm/1¼ inches in diameter. Space the spoonfuls about 5 cm/2 inches apart to allow for expansion.

4. Bake in the preheated oven for 10 minutes, or until risen and firm to the touch, switching over the baking trays halfway through cooking. Leave on the trays for 5 minutes, then transfer to a wire rack to cool.

5. For the filling, put the cream cheese, unsalted butter, vanilla and icing sugar in a mixing bowl and beat together with an electric handheld whisk until smooth and creamy. Beat in the boiling water to soften. Sandwich the whoopie pies together in pairs with the filling. Leave in a cool place to firm up for a couple of hours, then dust with icing sugar.

Mini Pies

Shortcrust pastry or pie dough

Makes: 625 g/1 lb 6 oz, or
enough for 12 muffin
sized pies, or 1 quantity
Prep: 25 minutes

350 g/12 oz plain flour, plus
extra for dusting

55 g/2 oz caster sugar, optional

85 g/3 oz unsalted butter,
chilled and diced

85 g/3 oz vegetable
shortening, chilled and diced

4–4½ tbsp cold water

The most versatile, everyday pastry, this is great for sweet pies — or simply omit the sugar for savoury tarts. Mix by hand or blitz in a food processor. The key is to use just enough water to bind the pastry for a wonderful crumbly texture that melts in the mouth.

1. To make by hand: put the flour and sugar (if making sweet shortcrust) in a mixing bowl, then add the butter and shortening. Toss together, then lift the mixture and rub it through your fingers and thumbs. Continue scooping up the mixture and rubbing until it looks like breadcrumbs. Gradually mix in the water with a round-bladed knife, then squeeze the mixture together with your hands until it forms a smooth dough.

To make with an electric mixer or food processor: put the flour, sugar, butter and shortening in a bowl and mix together using the electric mixer, or add to a processor bowl fitted with a plastic or metal blade and mix briefly. It should resemble breadcrumbs. Gradually add the water with the machine running and mix briefly until it just comes together in a ball.

2. Wrap the pastry in clingfilm or put it into a small plastic bag, and chill in the fridge for 15 minutes. Knead the pastry lightly on a surface dusted with flour, then roll it out thinly. Using a plain or fluted cookie cutter, stamp out circles 10 cm/4 inches in diameter and use to line a 12-section deep muffin tin. Alternatively stamp out circles 6 cm/2½ inches in diameter and use to line 2 x 12-section mini muffin tins. When you can cut no more circles, squeeze the trimmings into a ball, then reroll this out and cut round lids, strips for lattice tops or tiny shapes.

Tips

Keep everything as cold as possible. Use butter and vegetable shortening straight from the fridge. If your hands feel hot, rinse them in cold water before you begin. Use cold water to bind. A marble pastry board is useful (but not essential) for keeping the pastry cold while rolling out.

Don't add too much liquid. Use just enough to bind the crumbs. For shortcrust/pie dough you need 1 teaspoon of water for every 25 g/1 oz of mixture. For larger quantities change to tablespoons (1 tablespoon = 3 teaspoons). If you use too much water, the pastry will be hard.

Avoid over-flouring the work surface. Aim for the lightest of dustings and rub a little flour over the rolling pin. Before turning the pastry, loosen it with a long flexible palette knife.

All butter pastry

Makes: 650 g/1 lb 7 oz, or enough for 12 muffin sized pies, or 1 quantity

Prep: 25 minutes

350 g/12 oz plain flour, plus extra for dusting

85 g/3 oz icing sugar

175 g/6 oz unsalted butter, at room temperature, diced

4 egg yolks

Based on French 'pâte sucrée', this pastry has a higher ratio of sugar than shortcrust, is made with all butter and bound with egg yolks for richness.

1. To make by hand: spoon the flour on to the work surface, then sprinkle the sugar over the top. Mix together, then make a well in the centre and add the butter and yolks. Work the butter and yolks together with the fingers of one hand. Gradually draw in a little flour, working your fingertips in a circular motion but being careful not to let the yolk escape through the flour; use your other hand to flick a little flour around the edges so the yolks stay contained. Blend until almost all of the flour has been incorporated, then knead in the last bits until you have a smooth ball.

To make with an electric mixer or food processor: put the sugar and butter in a bowl and mix together using the electric mixer, or add to a processor bowl fitted with a plastic or metal blade and mix briefly. Add the egg yolks and a little of the flour and beat until smooth, then add the remaining flour and mix to make a smooth dough.

2. Wrap in clingfilm or put into a small plastic bag, chill in the fridge for 15 minutes, then roll out and shape as in point 2 of the method on page 68.

Tips
This pastry requires careful handling. Always chill it when it is first made, and again when it is shaped. If it is too soft to roll out, roll it out thinly between 2 sheets of baking paper.

Variations for Shortcrust and All butter pastry

Cinnamon:	Add 1 teaspoon of ground cinnamon with the sugar.
Chocolate:	Make with 325 g/11½ oz plain flour and 25 g/1 oz sifted cocoa powder.
Hazelnut:	Toast 55 g/2 oz hazelnuts until golden. Chop them finely and add with the sugar.
Lemon/Orange:	Add grated rind of 1 lemon or orange with the sugar.

Summer fruit pies

Makes: 24 mini muffin sized pies
Prep: 30 minutes
Cook: 15 minutes

a little butter, for greasing

350 g/12 oz mixed strawberries,
raspberries and redcurrants

2 tsp cornflour

3 tbsp caster sugar, plus extra for
sprinkling

grated rind of ½ lemon

450 g/1 lb Sweet Shortcrust
Pastry (see page 68) or
ready-made sweet shortcrust
pastry, chilled

a little plain flour, for dusting

1 egg yolk mixed with 1 tbsp
water, to glaze

whipped cream, to serve

Celebrate the summer with these gorgeous red fruit pies. The soft fruit contrasts deliciously with the crisp pastry.

1. Preheat the oven to 180°C/350°F/Gas Mark 4. Lightly grease 2 x 12-section mini muffin tins.

2. Roughly chop the strawberries and break up large raspberries. Put all the fruit in a mixing bowl and stir in the cornflour, sugar and lemon rind.

3. Roll the pastry out thinly on a lightly floured surface. Using a fluted cookie cutter, stamp out 24 circles, each 6 cm/2½ inches in diameter. Press these gently into the prepared tins, rerolling the trimmings as needed. Reserve some of the trimmings for decoration.

4. Brush the top edges of the pie cases with a little of the egg glaze, then spoon in the filling.

5. Roll the reserved pastry out thinly on a lightly floured surface. Cut strips 1 cm/½ inch wide. Arrange 2 strips over each pie, pressing the edges together well to seal, then use a cookie cutter to cut small stars and arrange these over the strips. Brush egg glaze over the pastry and sprinkle with a little sugar.

6. Bake in the preheated oven for 15 minutes, or until golden. Leave to cool in the tins for 10 minutes, then loosen with a round-bladed knife and transfer to a wire rack to cool. Serve warm or cold with whipped cream.

Valentine berry love pies

Makes: 24 mini muffin sized pies
Prep: 30 minutes
Cook: 15 minutes

a little butter, for greasing

350 g/12 oz strawberries

2 tsp cornflour

2 tbsp strawberry jam

grated rind of 2 limes

450 g/1 lb All Butter Pastry
(see page 69) or ready-made
sweet shortcrust pastry,
chilled

a little plain flour, for dusting

1 egg yolk mixed with 1 tbsp
water, to glaze

a little caster sugar, for
sprinkling

TO SERVE

225 ml/8 fl oz double cream

grated rind of 2 limes

2 tbsp icing sugar

These dainty pies are delicious while warm. If you can find a passion fruit in the shops, cut it in half and scoop out the seeds over the whipped cream topping just before serving.

1. Preheat the oven to 180°C/350°F/Gas Mark 4. Lightly grease 2 x 12-section mini muffin tins.

2. Roughly chop the strawberries. Put them in a mixing bowl and stir in the cornflour, jam and lime rind.

3. Roll half the pastry out thinly on a lightly floured surface. Using a fluted cookie cutter, stamp out 24 circles, each 6 cm/2½ inches in diameter. Press these gently into the prepared tins, rerolling the trimmings as needed.

4. Brush the top edges of the pie cases with a little of the egg glaze, then spoon in the filling.

5. Roll the reserved pastry out thinly on a lightly floured surface. Stamp out 24 circles, each 5 cm/2 inches in diameter, rerolling the trimmings as needed. Use a cookie cutter to cut hearts from each circle, some tiny, some bigger. Use the rounds and bigger hearts as lids, pressing the edges together. Brush egg glaze over the pastry and sprinkle with caster sugar.

6. Bake in the preheated oven for 15 minutes, or until golden. Leave to cool in the tins for 10 minutes, then loosen with a round-bladed knife and transfer to a wire rack to cool. Whip the cream until it forms soft swirls, then fold in half the lime rind and all the icing sugar. Sprinkle with the rest of the lime rind. Serve spoonfuls of the cream with the pies.

Deep South cherry pies

Makes: 24 mini muffin sized pies
Prep: 30 minutes
Cook: 15 minutes

a little butter, for greasing

350 g/12 oz cherries, stoned and halved, plus extra to decorate

2 tsp cornflour

3 tbsp caster sugar

1 tsp vanilla extract

½ tsp ground cinnamon

450 g/1 lb Sweet Shortcrust Pastry (see page 68) or ready-made sweet shortcrust pastry, chilled

a little plain flour, for dusting

1 egg yolk mixed with 1 tbsp water, to glaze

2 tbsp caster sugar mixed with a large pinch ground cinnamon, for sprinkling

These are sure to evoke happy memories of childhood. They're delicious served still hot from the oven with a drizzle of custard or spoonful of vanilla ice cream.

1. Preheat the oven to 180°C/350°F/Gas Mark 4. Lightly grease 2 x 12-section mini muffin tins.

2. Put the stoned cherries in a mixing bowl and stir in the cornflour, sugar, vanilla extract and cinnamon.

3. Roll two-thirds of the pastry out thinly on a lightly floured surface. Using a fluted cookie cutter, stamp out 24 circles, each 6 cm/2½ inches in diameter. Press these into the prepared tins, rerolling the trimmings as needed.

4. Brush the top edges of the pie cases with a little of the egg glaze, then spoon in the filling.

5. Roll the reserved pastry out thinly on a lightly floured surface. Stamp out 24 circles, each 5 cm/2 inches in diameter, rerolling the trimmings as needed. Arrange these on top of the pies, pressing the edges together to seal. Brush over some egg glaze. Use a cookie cutter to cut tiny hearts and flowers from the remaining pastry and arrange these on the lids. Brush egg glaze over the decorations.

6. Bake in the preheated oven for 15 minutes, or until golden. Leave to cool in the tins for 10 minutes, then loosen with a round-bladed knife and transfer to a wire rack to cool. Serve warm or cold, sprinkled with the cinnamon mixture, on a plate decorated with extra cherries.

Peach and chocolate meringue pies

Makes: 6 muffin sized pies
Prep: 40 minutes
Cook: 22–25 minutes

What is there not to like? Crisp hazelnut pastry with a slightly tart peach filling that contrasts with a soft cloud of sweet meringue swirled with melted dark chocolate. You don't need to add anything, not even cream.

225 g/8 oz All Butter Hazelnut Pastry (see page 69) or ready-made sweet shortcrust pastry, chilled

a little plain flour, for dusting

25 g/1 oz butter, plus extra for greasing

2 peaches, peeled if liked, halved, stoned and diced

50 g/1¾ oz dark chocolate, roughly chopped

2 egg whites

55 g/2 oz caster sugar

1. Lightly grease a 6-section muffin tin. Roll the pastry out thinly on a lightly floured surface. Using a plain cookie cutter, stamp out 6 circles each 10 cm/4 inches in diameter. Press these gently into the prepared tin, rerolling the trimmings as needed. Prick the base of each pie with a fork, then chill in the fridge for 15 minutes. Preheat the oven to 190°C/375°F/Gas Mark 5.

2. Line the pastry cases with squares of crumpled baking paper and fill with baking beans. Bake in the preheated oven for 10 minutes. Remove the paper and beans and cook the pastry cases for 2–3 minutes more, or until the base of the pastry is crisp and dry.

3. Meanwhile, melt the butter in a small frying pan or saucepan, add the peaches and cook gently for 5 minutes, stirring occasionally, until softened. Spoon the peaches into the pastry cases.

4. Put the chocolate in a heatproof bowl, set over a saucepan of gently simmering water and heat until melted. Whisk the egg whites in a large clean mixing bowl until you have stiff, moist-looking peaks, then gradually whisk in the sugar a teaspoon at a time for another 1–2 minutes, or until the meringue is very thick and glossy. Fold the melted chocolate into the meringue with just a couple of swirls of the spoon for a marbled effect. Spoon into the pies.

5. Bake in the preheated oven for 5–7 minutes, or until the meringue peaks are golden and just cooked through. Leave to cool in the tin for 10 minutes, then loosen with a round-bladed knife and transfer to a wire rack to cool. Serve warm.

Brandy apple pies

Makes: 24 mini muffin sized pies
Prep: 35 minutes
Cook: 23–25 minutes

These dainty little high-topped pies have been personalized by adding an initial made from a tiny rope of pastry for each of your dinner guests; if you have a set of little alphabet cutters then you may prefer to use these. If you wish, cook these pies in advance and freeze when cool, then warm through when needed.

450 g/1 lb cooking apples, quartered, cored, peeled and diced

25 g/1 oz butter, plus extra for greasing

55 g/2 oz caster sugar, plus extra for sprinkling

55 g/2 oz sultanas or raisins

grated rind of 1 lemon

3 tbsp brandy or Bourbon

1 quantity All Butter Pastry (see page 69) or ready-made sweet shortcrust pastry, chilled

a little plain flour, for dusting

a little milk, to glaze

whipped cream, to serve

1. Preheat the oven to 180°C/350°F/Gas Mark 4. Lightly grease 2 x 12-section mini muffin tins.

2. Put the apples in a medium saucepan with the butter, sugar, sultanas and lemon rind. Cook, uncovered, over a gentle heat, stirring from time to time, for 8–10 minutes, or until the apples have softened but still hold their shape. Add the brandy and cook until just bubbling. Keeping it over the heat, flame with a taper or long match, stand well back and cook for a minute or so, until the flame subsides. Leave the mixture to cool.

3. Roll half the pastry out thinly on a lightly floured surface. Using a fluted cookie cutter, stamp out 24 circles, each 6 cm/2½ inches in diameter. Press these gently into the prepared tins, rerolling the trimmings as needed.

4. Brush the top edges of the pie cases with milk, then spoon in the filling, doming it up high in the centre.

5. Roll the reserved pastry out thinly on a lightly floured surface. Stamp out 24 circles, the same size as before, rerolling the trimmings as needed. Arrange these on top of the pies, pressing the edges together well to seal. Brush milk over the pastry.

6. Shape tiny ropes from the remaining pastry into the initials of your dinner guests or family. Press these onto the pie tops, brush with a little extra milk and sprinkle with sugar.

7. Bake in the preheated oven for 15 minutes, or until golden. Leave to cool in the tins for 10 minutes, then loosen with a round-bladed knife and transfer to a wire rack to cool. Serve warm or cold, sprinkled with a little extra sugar, with spoonfuls of whipped cream.

Hot spiced pumpkin pies

Makes: 24 mini muffin sized pies
Prep: 30 minutes
Cook: 30 minutes

a little butter, for greasing

250 g/9 oz pumpkin (weighed
after deseeding and peeling),
diced small

4 tbsp semi-skimmed milk

2 eggs

3 tbsp runny honey

1 tsp ground ginger

¼ tsp ground mixed spice

325 g/11½ oz All Butter Pastry
(see page 69) or ready-made
sweet shortcrust pastry, chilled

a little plain flour, for dusting

a little milk, to glaze

a little caster sugar, for sprinkling

These are always popular for Halloween. Serve them as they are or top with a spoonful of whipped cream flavoured with a little honey or maple syrup.

1. Preheat the oven to 190°C/375°F/Gas Mark 5. Lightly grease 2 x 12-section mini muffin tins.

2. Put the pumpkin in a steamer, cover and set over a pan of gently simmering water. Steam for 15 minutes, or until tender. Purée with the milk in a liquidizer or food processor until smooth. Cool slightly, then mix in the eggs, honey, ginger and mixed spice.

3. Roll the pastry out thinly on a lightly floured surface. Using a plain cookie cutter, stamp out 24 circles, each 6 cm/2½ inches in diameter. Press these gently into the tins, rerolling the trimmings as needed. Squeeze any remaining trimmings together and reserve.

4. Brush the top edges of the pie cases with milk, then spoon in the filling.

5. Roll the remaining pastry trimmings out thinly on a lightly floured surface. Use a sharp knife to cut tiny leaves and mark on veins. Brush these with milk, arrange them over each pie and sprinkle with a little sugar.

6. Bake in the preheated oven for 15 minutes, or until the leaves are golden and the filling is just set. Leave to cool in the tins for 10 minutes, then loosen with a round-bladed knife and transfer to a wire rack to cool. Serve warm or cold, sprinkled with a little extra sugar.

Christmas cranberry and orange pies

Makes: 12 mini muffin sized pies
Prep: 30 minutes
Cook: 30 minutes

Cranberries needn't be kept just for sauce to go with the turkey; try them gently poached with star anise for a fragrant filling in an orange-scented pie crust. The secret to cooking cranberries is not to add sugar at first, but instead when the skins have softened. For a festive accompaniment serve with whipped cream flavoured with orange liqueur.

a little butter, for greasing

175 g/6 oz frozen cranberries

1 tbsp cornflour

3 tbsp freshly squeezed orange juice

2 star anise

55 g/2 oz caster sugar, plus extra for sprinkling

225 g/8 oz Orange Sweet Shortcrust Pastry (see pages 68–69) or ready-made sweet shortcrust pastry, chilled

a little plain flour, for dusting

a little milk, to glaze

a little caster sugar, for sprinkling

1. Preheat the oven to 180°C/350°F/Gas Mark 4. Lightly grease a 12-section mini muffin tin.

2. Put the still-frozen cranberries in a medium saucepan with the cornflour and orange juice. Add the star anise and cook uncovered over a low heat, stirring from time to time, for 5 minutes, or until the cranberries have softened. Add the sugar and cook for 5 minutes more, then leave to cool.

3. Roll the pastry out thinly on a lightly floured surface. Using a fluted cookie cutter, stamp out 12 circles, each 6 cm/2½ inches in diameter. Press these gently into the prepared tin, rerolling the trimmings as needed. Squeeze any remaining trimmings together and reserve.

4. Brush the top edges of the pie cases with a little milk. Discard the star anise, then spoon in the filling.

5. Roll the remaining pastry out thinly on a lightly floured surface. Using a fluted pastry wheel, cut thin strips of pastry. Arrange these over each pie and brush with a little milk. Sprinkle with a little sugar. Bake in the preheated oven for 20 minutes, covering with foil after 10 minutes if the tops are browning too quickly. Leave to cool in the tin for 10 minutes, then loosen with a round-bladed knife and transfer to a wire rack to cool. Serve warm or cold.

Shaker lemon pies

Makes: 24 mini muffin sized pies
Prep: 40 minutes
Cook: 55 minutes

These are traditionally made with thin-skinned Meyer lemons soaked for hours in sugar before baking, but as they are notoriously difficult to find, ordinary lemons have been used here instead. To get around the increased bitterness, two lemons are thinly sliced and poached in a sugar syrup, then mixed with extra grated lemon rind and juice for a tangy filling.

3½ medium lemons

250 g/9 oz caster sugar, plus extra for sprinkling

4 tbsp water

60 g/2¼ oz butter, plus extra for greasing

3 eggs

450 g/1 lb All Butter Pastry (see page 69) or ready-made sweet shortcrust pastry, chilled

a little plain flour, for dusting

egg white, to glaze

1. Lightly grease 2 x 12-section mini muffin tins. Thinly slice 2 of the lemons – you need 24 slices. Put them in a medium saucepan with 100 g/3½ oz the sugar and the water and stir. Cook uncovered over a low heat, stirring from time to time, for 30 minutes, or until the lemon slices are soft and translucent and only just beginning to lose their colour. Using a fork, scoop the lemon slices out of the saucepan, draining off the syrup, and put them on a plate; they will be used in step 5.

2. Preheat the oven to 180°C/350°F/Gas Mark 4. Grate the rind and squeeze the juice from the remaining lemons. Add them to the syrup with the butter and remaining sugar. Heat gently, uncovered, until the butter is just melted.

3. Meanwhile, beat the eggs in a small bowl. Remove the pan from the heat and strain the eggs through a sieve into it, stirring well. Return to the heat and cook very gently for 10 minutes, stirring frequently, or until the mixture has thickened and is jam-like. Increase the heat if needed but keep a watchful eye; too hot and the eggs will curdle. Leave to cool.

4. Roll half the pastry out thinly on a lightly floured surface. Using a fluted cookie cutter, stamp out 24 circles, each 6 cm/2½ inches in diameter. Press these gently into the prepared tins, rerolling trimmings as needed.

5. Brush the top edges of the cases with a little egg white, then spoon in the filling. Top each with a slice of the candied lemon made in step 1.

6. Roll the reserved pastry out thinly on a lightly floured surface. Stamp out 24 circles, each 5 cm/2 inches in diameter, rerolling the trimmings as needed. Press these onto the pie tops, pressing the edges together well.

7. Make 4 small cuts in the top of each pie, brush the pies with egg white and sprinkle with sugar. Bake in the preheated oven for 15 minutes, or until golden. Leave to cool in the tins for 10 minutes, then loosen with a round-bladed knife and transfer to a wire rack to cool. Serve warm or cold.

Lemon meringue pies

Makes: 12 muffin sized pies
Prep: 30 minutes
Cook: 18–22 minutes

100 g/3½ oz butter, plus extra for greasing

2 tbsp golden syrup

300 g/10½ oz digestive biscuits, crushed

grated rind and juice of 3 lemons

200 g/7 oz caster sugar

40 g/1½ oz cornflour

3 eggs, separated

This all-time classic is loved by everyone, with its sharp tangy lemon filling topped generously with piped or spooned meringue. These are made with a crumb crust.

1. Preheat the oven to 180°C/350°F/Gas Mark 4. Lightly grease a 12-section muffin tin.

2. Put the butter and syrup in a small saucepan and heat until the butter has just melted. Take the pan off the heat, stir in the biscuit crumbs, then divide the mixture between the sections of the prepared tin. Press it firmly over the base and sides of the tin with the back of a teaspoon.

3. Line the cases with baking paper and fill with baking beans, then bake them in the preheated oven for 8–10 minutes, or until slightly darker in colour. Leave to cool and harden in the tin for 10–15 minutes. Remove the paper and beans.

4. Put the lemon rind in a second, slightly larger saucepan. Make the juice up to 450 ml/16 fl oz with cold water, then add this liquid to the rind and bring just to the boil. In a mixing bowl, stir 85 g/3 oz sugar, the cornflour and egg yolks together until a thick paste has formed, then gradually stir in the boiling lemon juice until smooth.

5. Pour the liquid back into the saucepan and cook over a medium heat, stirring constantly, for a few minutes, until it is very thick and smooth. Spoon the filling into the crumb cases.

6. For the topping, whisk the egg whites in a large clean mixing bowl until you have stiff peaks, then gradually whisk in the remaining sugar a teaspoon at a time for another 1–2 minutes, or until the meringue is very thick and glossy. Spoon or pipe the meringue on top of the pies.

7. Bake in the preheated oven for 10–12 minutes, or until the meringue peaks are golden and just cooked through. Leave to cool and firm up in the tin, then loosen with a round-bladed knife and transfer to a plate.

S'more pies

Makes: 12 mini muffin sized pies
Prep: 20 minutes
Cook: 9–10 minutes

This summer camp favourite gets the grown-up treatment. Mini crumb cases flavoured with peanut butter, then filled with a rich dark chocolate cream and piled high with mini marshmallows. Great with cups of strong coffee or hot chocolate at the end of a barbecue.

40 g/1½ oz butter, plus extra for greasing

1 tbsp crunchy peanut butter

85 g/3 oz Rich Tea biscuits, crushed

100 g/3½ oz plain chocolate, roughly chopped

1 tbsp icing sugar

6 tbsp double cream

40 g/1½ oz mini marshmallows

1. Preheat the oven to 180°C/350°F/Gas Mark 4. Lightly grease a 12-section mini muffin tin.

2. Put the butter in a small saucepan. Gently heat, uncovered, until it has melted. Take the saucepan off the heat and stir in the peanut butter, then the biscuit crumbs. Divide between the sections of the prepared tin. Press it firmly over the base and sides of the tin with the back of a teaspoon.

3. Bake in the preheated oven for 6 minutes, or until slightly darker in colour. Reshape the centre if needed with the back of a spoon. Leave to cool and harden in the tin for 10–15 minutes.

4. Meanwhile, put the chocolate in a heatproof bowl, set the bowl over a saucepan of gently simmering water and heat until melted. Add the sugar and gradually stir in the cream until smooth. Preheat the grill to medium.

5. Spoon the filling into the cases. Sprinkle the mini marshmallows over the top and press them lightly into the chocolate so they don't roll off.

6. Grill for 3–4 minutes, or until the marshmallows have softened and are just beginning to colour. Leave to cool in the tin for 30 minutes, then loosen with a round-bladed knife and carefully lift out of the tin. Serve.

Blueberry tarts

Makes: 24 mini muffin sized pies
Prep: 25 minutes
Cook: 17–18 minutes

300 g/10½ oz blueberries

2 tsp cornflour

55 g/2 oz caster sugar

4 tsp water

55 g/2 oz plain flour, plus extra
for dusting

grated rind of 1 lemon

40 g/1½ oz butter, diced, plus
extra for greasing

325 g/11½ oz All Butter Pastry
(see page 69) or ready-made
sweet shortcrust pastry, chilled

Crisp, dainty pies with a moist blueberry filling and a buttery crumble top. Serve while still warm, with good vanilla ice cream.

1. Preheat the oven to 190°C/375°F/Gas Mark 5. Lightly grease 2 x 12-section mini muffin tins.

2. Put half the blueberries in a small saucepan with the cornflour, half the caster sugar and the water. Cook, uncovered, over a medium heat, stirring constantly, for 2–3 minutes, or until the juices begin to run and the sauce thickens. Take the pan off the heat and add the remaining blueberries.

3. For the streusel, put the flour, lemon rind, butter and remaining sugar in a medium mixing bowl. Toss together, then lift the mixture and rub it through your fingers and thumbs until it looks like fine breadcrumbs.

4. Roll the pastry out thinly on a lightly floured surface. Using a fluted cookie cutter, stamp out 24 circles each 6 cm/2½ inches in diameter. Press these into the prepared tins, rerolling trimmings as needed. Spoon the blueberry filling into the cases, then sprinkle the tops of the tarts with the streusel mixture.

5. Bake in the preheated oven for 15 minutes, or until the topping is pale gold. Leave to cool in the tins for 10 minutes, then loosen with a round-bladed knife and transfer to a wire rack to cool. Serve warm or cold.

Orchard tarts

Makes: 6 muffin sized pies
Prep: 45 minutes
Cook: 32–33 minutes

a little butter, for greasing

225 g/8 oz All Butter Pastry (see page 69) or ready-made sweet shortcrust pastry, chilled

a little plain flour, for dusting

1 pear, about 150 g/5½ oz, quartered, cored, peeled and diced

1 cooking apple, about 150 g/5½ oz, quartered, cored, peeled and diced

3 ripe red plums, halved, stoned and diced

25 g/1 oz caster sugar

1 tbsp water

1 tbsp sunflower oil

1 tbsp runny honey

4 tbsp porridge oats

1 tbsp sesame seeds

2 tbsp sunflower seeds

2 tbsp pumpkin seeds

2 tbsp hazelnuts, roughly chopped

Apple pies with a twist; they are sprinkled with homemade granola (a mix of oats, seeds and nuts). Mix and match the topping ingredients to suit your larder; try barley flakes, flaked almonds, chopped macadamia nuts, golden linseeds or pumpkin seeds.

1. Lightly grease a 6-section muffin tin. Roll the pastry out thinly on a lightly floured surface. Using a plain cookie cutter, stamp out 6 circles each 10 cm/4 inches in diameter. Press these gently into the prepared tin, rerolling the trimmings as needed. Prick the base of each with a fork, then chill in the fridge for 15 minutes. Preheat the oven to 190°C/375°F/Gas Mark 5.

2. Line the pastry cases with squares of crumpled baking paper and fill with baking beans. Bake in the preheated oven for 10 minutes. Remove the paper and beans and cook the cases for 2–3 minutes more, or until the base of the pastry is crisp and dry. Turn the oven down to 180°C/350°F/Gas Mark 4.

3. Put all the fruit, sugar and water in a medium saucepan. Cover and cook over a gentle heat, stirring, for 5 minutes, or until the fruit has just softened. Meanwhile, for the granola, warm the oil and honey in a frying pan. Stir in the oats, seeds and hazelnuts and set aside. Spoon the fruit into the cases, then sprinkle the granola on top.

4. Bake in the preheated oven for 20 minutes, covering with foil after 10 minutes if the granola is browning too quickly. Leave to cool in the tin for 10 minutes, then loosen with a round-bladed knife and transfer to a wire rack to cool. Serve warm.

Caramelized apple tarts

Makes: 12 muffin sized pies
Prep: 45 minutes
Cook: 32–36 minutes

These French-inspired tarts are filled with a tangy apple and lemon custard, then topped with wafer-thin sliced apples and glazed with a little icing sugar. They can be tricky to remove from the tin as the sugar glaze makes them sticky, so do take extra care.

450 g/1 lb Sweet Shortcrust Pastry (see page 68) or ready-made sweet shortcrust pastry, chilled

a little plain flour, for dusting

5 Granny Smith apples, quartered, cored and peeled

85 g/3 oz caster sugar

finely grated rind and juice of 1 lemon

2 eggs

15 g/½ oz butter, plus extra for greasing

3 tbsp icing sugar, sifted

1. Lightly grease a 12-section muffin tin. Roll the pastry out thinly on a lightly floured surface. Using a plain cookie cutter, stamp out 12 circles, each 10 cm/4 inches in diameter. Press these gently into the prepared tin, rerolling the trimmings as needed. Prick the base of each with a fork, then chill in the fridge for 15 minutes. Preheat the oven to 190°C/375°F/Gas Mark 5.

2. Line the pastry cases with squares of crumpled baking paper and fill with baking beans. Bake in the preheated oven for 10 minutes. Remove the paper and beans and cook the cases for 2–3 minutes more, or until the base of the pastry is crisp and dry. Turn the oven down to 180°C/350°F/Gas Mark 4.

3. Roughly grate 8 of the apple quarters into a mixing bowl. Add two thirds of the caster sugar, all the lemon rind and juice and the eggs and whisk together. Spoon the filling into the cases.

4. Thinly slice the remaining apples and arrange them overlapping on top of the pies. Sprinkle with the remaining caster sugar and then dot the pies with the butter.

5. Bake in the preheated oven for 20–25 minutes, or until the filling is set and the sliced apples are browned around the edges.

6. Dust with the icing sugar and return the pies to the oven for 5 minutes, or until the sugar has caramelized. Leave to cool in the tin for 15 minutes, then loosen with a round-bladed knife and transfer to a wire rack to cool. Serve warm or cold.

Mississippi mud pies

Makes: 6 muffin sized pies
Prep: 30 minutes
Cook: 12–13 minutes

a little butter, for greasing

225 g/8 oz Chocolate or Hazelnut
Sweet Shortcrust Pastry
(see pages 68–69) or ready-made
sweet shortcrust pastry, chilled

a little plain flour, for dusting

100 g/3½ oz plain chocolate,
roughly chopped

4 tbsp icing sugar

125 ml/4 fl oz semi-skimmed milk

1 egg

225 ml/8 fl oz double cream

1 tsp vanilla extract

white and dark chocolate curls,
to decorate

A dark, rich, almost truffle-like chocolate layer encased in an even darker crisp chocolate pastry, then topped with soft swirls of Chantilly cream.

1. Lightly grease a 6-section muffin tin. Roll the pastry out thinly on a lightly floured surface. Using a plain cookie cutter, stamp out 6 circles each 10 cm/4 inches in diameter. Press these gently into the prepared tin, rerolling the trimmings as needed. Prick the base of each with a fork, then chill in the fridge for 15 minutes. Preheat the oven to 190°C/375°F/Gas Mark 5.

2. Line the pastry cases with squares of crumpled baking paper and fill with baking beans. Bake in the preheated oven for 10 minutes. Remove the paper and beans and cook the cases for 2–3 minutes more, or until the base of the pastry is crisp and dry.

3. Meanwhile, put the plain chocolate in a heatproof bowl, set the bowl over a saucepan of gently simmering water and heat until melted. Beat 2 tablespoons of sugar, the milk and egg together in a jug. Take the bowl of chocolate off the heat and gradually stir in the milk mixture until smooth. Pour the filling into the cases and leave to cool. Transfer the pies to the fridge for 2 hours, or until the filling has set.

4. Whip the cream with the remaining icing sugar and the vanilla until it forms soft folds. Loosen the pastry cases with a round-bladed knife and lift them onto a plate. Spoon the cream over the top and decorate with the chocolate curls.

Chocolate and pecan tarts

Makes: 24 mini muffin sized pies
Prep: 25 minutes
Cook: 20 minutes

115 g/4 oz golden syrup

70 g/2½ oz light muscovado sugar

25 g/1 oz butter, plus extra for greasing

50 g/1¾ oz dark chocolate, roughly chopped

325 g/11½ oz All Butter Cinnamon Pastry (see page 69) or ready-made sweet shortcrust pastry, chilled

a little plain flour, for dusting

1 egg, beaten

1 egg yolk

85 g/3 oz pecan nuts

50 g/1¾ oz dark chocolate, roughly chopped, to decorate

These pies freeze well packed into a plastic box. Once defrosted, add a dusting of icing sugar and a drizzle of melted chocolate before serving. Alternatively, warm them in the oven and serve with whipped cream flavoured with ground cinnamon or Greek yogurt and honey.

1. Preheat the oven to 180°C/350°F/Gas Mark 4. Lightly grease a 2 x 12-section mini muffin tins.

2. Put the syrup, sugar and butter in a small saucepan. Heat gently, uncovered, stirring from time to time, until the butter has just melted. Add the chocolate and stir until it too has melted. Leave to cool slightly.

3. Roll the pastry out thinly on a lightly floured surface. Using a fluted cookie cutter, stamp out 24 circles each 6 cm/2½ inches in diameter. Press these gently into the prepared tins, rerolling the trimmings as needed.

4. Stir the egg and egg yolk into the cooled chocolate mixture until smooth, then spoon this filling into the cases. Decorate the top of each pie with 2 pecan nuts.

5. Bake in the preheated oven for 20 minutes, or until the filling has set, and covering with foil after 10 minutes if the nuts are browning too quickly. Leave to cool in the tins for 10 minutes, then loosen with a round-bladed knife and transfer to a wire rack to cool.

6. For the decoration, put the chocolate in a heatproof bowl, set the bowl over a saucepan of gently simmering water and heat until melted. Dust the tops of the pies with a little sifted icing sugar. Spoon the chocolate into a paper piping bag, snip off the tip and pipe zigzag lines of melted chocolate over the pies, or drizzle the chocolate from a teaspoon. Leave the pies to set for 10 minutes, then arrange on a serving plate.

Pistachio and almond tarts

Makes: 12 mini muffin sized pies
Prep: 20 minutes
Cook: 15 minutes

225 g/8 oz Sweet Shortcrust
Pastry (see page 68) or
ready-made sweet shortcrust
pastry, chilled

a little plain flour, for dusting

50 g/1¾ oz butter, softened, plus
extra for greasing

50 g/1¾ oz caster sugar

1 egg yolk

50 g/1¾ oz ground almonds

a few drops of almond extract or
orange flower water

1½ tbsp flaked almonds

1 tbsp pistachio nuts, thinly sliced

a little icing sugar, sifted, to
decorate

A true French frangipane is made with just almonds, but a mixture of pretty green-tinged sliced pistachios and ground and flaked almonds makes for a luxurious mini pie.

1. Lightly grease a 12-section mini muffin tin. Preheat the oven to 180°C/350°F/Gas Mark 4.

2. Roll the pastry out thinly on a lightly floured surface. Using a fluted cookie cutter, stamp out 12 circles each 6 cm/2½ inches in diameter. Press these gently into the prepared tin, rerolling the trimmings as needed.

3. Meanwhile, put the butter and caster sugar in a mixing bowl and beat together until light and fluffy. Beat in the egg yolk, then the ground almonds. Flavour with a little almond essence or orange flower water.

4. Spoon the frangipane into the pastry cases.

5. Sprinkle the flaked almonds and sliced pistachios over the top and press them lightly into the filling.

6. Bake in the preheated oven for 15 minutes, or until the almonds are golden. Leave to cool in the tin for 10 minutes, then loosen with a round-bladed knife and transfer to a wire rack to cool. Serve warm or cold, dusted with sifted icing sugar.

Coffee tarts

Makes: 12 muffin sized pies
Prep: 40 minutes
Cook: 27–33 minutes

Dark, rich and not too sweet. Bite through a crisp buttery pie case to a coffee and dark chocolate custard, topped with whipped cream, flavoured with coffee cream liqueur. Delicious served with a cup of strong black coffee.

a little butter, for greasing

450 g/1 lb All Butter Pastry (see page 69) or ready-made sweet shortcrust pastry, chilled

a little plain flour, for dusting

225 ml/8 fl oz semi-skimmed milk

115 g/4 oz plain chocolate, roughly chopped

2 tsp instant coffee powder or granules

2 tbsp caster sugar

2 eggs

2 egg yolks

DECORATION

200 ml/7 fl oz double cream

2 tbsp icing sugar

2 tbsp coffee cream liqueur

1½ tsp instant coffee dissolved in 1 tsp boiling water

white chocolate curls, to decorate

a dusting of cocoa, sifted, to decorate

1. Lightly grease a 12-section muffin tin. Roll the pastry out thinly on a lightly floured surface. Using a plain cookie cutter, stamp out 12 circles each 10 cm/4 inches in diameter. Press these gently into the prepared tin, rerolling the trimmings as needed. Prick the base of each with a fork, then chill for 15 minutes. Preheat the oven to 190°C/375°F/Gas Mark 5.

2. Line the pastry cases with squares of crumpled baking paper and fill with baking beans. Bake in the preheated oven for 10 minutes. Remove the paper and beans and cook the cases for 2–3 minutes more, or until the base of the pastry is crisp. Turn the oven down to 160°C/325°F/Gas Mark 3. Meanwhile, bring the milk just to the boil in a small saucepan. Add the chocolate, coffee and caster sugar and leave to stand, off the heat, until the chocolate has melted.

3. Beat the eggs and yolks in a mixing bowl, then gradually whisk in the warm milk mixture until smooth. Pour the custard into the pastry cases.

4. Bake in the preheated oven for 15–20 minutes, or until just set. Leave to cool in the tin for 10 minutes, then loosen with a round-bladed knife and transfer to a wire rack. Whip the cream in a bowl until it forms soft swirls. Add the sugar, then whisk in the liqueur and coffee until thick. Spoon over the pies, then decorate with white chocolate curls and a dusting of cocoa.

Cherry cream pies

Makes: 12 muffin sized pies
Prep: 30 minutes
Cook: 25–30 minutes

These light cheese pies are perfect for a special summer picnic, although you may need to pack them with a little crumpled foil or kitchen roll to cushion any knocks. Serve with a spoonful of whipped cream flavoured with a little sugar and vanilla.

a little butter, for greasing

300 g/10½ oz mascarpone cheese

2 tsp plain flour, plus extra for dusting

85 g/3 oz caster sugar, plus extra for sprinkling

2 eggs

6 tbsp natural yogurt

1 tsp vanilla extract

450 g/1 lb All Butter Pastry (see page 69) or ready-made sweet shortcrust pastry, chilled

a little milk, to glaze

36 fresh or canned cherries, stoned and drained well

1. Lightly grease a 12-section muffin tin. Preheat the oven to 180°C/350°F/Gas Mark 4.

2. Spoon the mascarpone cheese into a mixing bowl and add the flour, sugar, eggs, yogurt and vanilla. Beat with a wooden spoon or electric hand-held whisk until just mixed.

3. Roll the pastry out thinly on a lightly floured surface. Using a plain cookie cutter, stamp out 12 circles each 10 cm/4 inches in diameter. Press these gently into the prepared tin, rerolling the trimmings as needed and reserving any remaining pastry. Brush the top edges of the pie cases with a little of the milk glaze and spoon in the filling. Add 3 cherries to each pie.

4. Roll the reserved pastry out thinly on a lightly floured surface. Cut strips about 1-cm/½-inch wide. Arrange 4 strips over each pie to make a lattice, pressing the edges together well to seal, then brush milk over the pastry and sprinkle with a little sugar.

5. Bake in the preheated oven for 25–30 minutes, or until the lattice is golden and the filling is just set. Leave to cool in the tin for 10 minutes, then loosen with a round-bladed knife and transfer to a wire rack to cool. Serve at room temperature.

Key lime pies

Makes: 24 mini muffin sized pies
Prep: 15 minutes
Cook: 6–8 minutes

4 tbsp golden syrup

70 g/2½ oz butter, plus extra for greasing

175 g/6 oz digestive biscuits, crushed

150 ml/5 fl oz double cream

grated rind of 2 limes

200 g/7 oz canned sweetened condensed milk

4 tbsp freshly squeezed limes (about 2 limes)

extra lime zest, to decorate

These super-speedy mini pies are filled with a luscious no-bake citrusy cream sweetened with condensed milk. They're great to make with kids.

1. Preheat the oven to 180°C/350°F/Gas Mark 4. Lightly grease 2 x 12-section mini muffin tins.

2. Put the syrup and butter in a small saucepan. Heat gently, uncovered, stirring, until the butter has just melted. Take the saucepan off the heat and stir in the biscuit crumbs. Divide the mixture between the sections of the prepared tins. Press it firmly over the base and sides of the tins with the back of a teaspoon.

3. Bake in the preheated oven for 6 minutes, or until slightly darker in colour. Reshape the centre if needed with the back of a spoon. Leave to cool and harden in the tins for 10–15 minutes.

4. Meanwhile, pour the cream into a bowl, add the lime rind and whisk until it is beginning to thicken. Gradually whisk in the condensed milk, then the lime juice, whisking for a few minutes more until it has thickened.

5. Pipe or spoon the lime cream into the cases. Chill for 30 minutes, or longer if you have time. Loosen the pies with a round-bladed knife and lift them carefully out of the tins. Decorate with lime zest curls.

Maple cream pies with orange

Makes: 12 muffin sized pies
Prep: 45 minutes
Cook: 37–38 minutes

a little butter, for greasing

450 g/1 lb All Butter Pastry (see
page 69) or ready-made sweet
shortcrust pastry, chilled

a little plain flour, for dusting

225 ml/8 fl oz double cream

125 ml/4 fl oz maple syrup

2 eggs

2 egg yolks

grated rind of 1 orange

TO SERVE

3 oranges, peeled and segmented

3 tbsp maple syrup

Delicately flavoured creamy custard pies with a hint of maple and orange rind. Delicious served at room temperature, with extra orange segments and a drizzle of maple syrup.

1. Lightly grease a 12-section muffin tin. Roll the pastry out thinly on a lightly floured surface. Using a fluted cookie cutter, stamp out 12 circles, each 10 cm/4 inches in diameter. Press these gently into the prepared tin, rerolling the trimmings as needed. Prick the base of each with a fork, then chill in the fridge for 15 minutes. Preheat the oven to 190°C/375°F/Gas Mark 5.

2. Line the pastry cases with squares of crumpled baking paper and fill with baking beans. Bake in the preheated oven for 10 minutes. Remove the paper and beans and cook the pastry cases for 2–3 minutes more, or until the base of the pastry is crisp and dry. Turn the oven down to 160°C/325°F/ Gas Mark 3.

3. Whisk the cream, syrup, eggs, egg yolks and most of the orange rind together in a jug. Pour this filling into the pie cases.

4. Bake in the preheated oven for 25 minutes, or until the custard is set. Leave to cool in the tins for 10 minutes, then loosen with a round-bladed knife and transfer to a serving plate.

5. Serve topped with extra orange segments, a sprinkling of the remaining grated orange rind and a drizzle of maple syrup.

Honey, walnut and ricotta pies

Makes: 24 mini muffin sized pies
Prep: 45 minutes
Cook: 25 minutes

Made here with a crisp, rich, all butter pastry, these would also taste great with cinnamon shortcrust. The perfect pie for those who don't have a sweet tooth. Undecorated pies will keep in the fridge for two to three days.

a little butter, for greasing

a little olive oil, for greasing

325 g/11½ oz All Butter Pastry (see page 69) or ready-made sweet shortcrust pastry, chilled

a little plain flour, for dusting

125 g/4½ oz walnut pieces

225 g/8 oz ricotta cheese

2 egg yolks

5 tbsp runny orange blossom honey

a large pinch of ground cinnamon

115 g/4 oz granulated sugar

1 tbsp water

200 g/7 oz Greek yogurt, to serve

1. Lightly grease 2 x 12-section mini muffin tins and oil a baking tray. Preheat the oven to 180°C/350°F/Gas Mark 4.

2. Roll the pastry out thinly on a lightly floured surface. Using a fluted cookie cutter, stamp out 24 circles each 6 cm/2½ inches in diameter. Press these gently into the prepared tins, rerolling the trimmings as needed.

3. Lightly toast half the walnut pieces in a dry non-stick frying pan. Leave them to cool, then roughly chop them.

4. Lightly whisk the ricotta, egg yolks, 4 tablespoons of the honey and the cinnamon together in a mixing bowl until just mixed. Stir in the toasted walnuts. Spoon the filling into the cases.

5. Bake in the preheated oven for 20 minutes, or until the filling is golden brown. Leave in the tin for 10 minutes to cool.

6. Meanwhile, for the praline put the sugar, remaining 1 tablespoon of honey and the water into the frying pan and heat gently without stirring until the sugar has dissolved. Tilt the pan to mix any remaining grains of sugar into the syrup. Add the remaining walnuts and cook over a medium heat, again without stirring, for about 5 minutes, or until the syrup turns a rich golden brown. Keep a watchful eye on the syrup as it will suddenly begin to change colour, darkening first around the edges. Tilt the pan to mix if needed, then quickly pour the praline onto the prepared baking tray and leave to cool and harden.

7. Loosen the pies with a round-bladed knife and transfer them to a plate. Just before serving, top them with spoonfuls of yogurt. Loosen the praline from the baking tray with a knife, then break or cut it into thin shards and press pieces of it into the yogurt.

Coconut cream pies

Makes: 12 muffin sized pies
Prep: 40 minutes
Cook: 8–10 minutes

2 tbsp golden syrup

100 g/3½ oz butter, plus extra for greasing

300 g/10½ oz gingersnap or digestive biscuits, crushed

85 g/3 oz unsweetened desiccated coconut

125 ml/4 fl oz boiling water

55 g/2 oz caster sugar

20 g/¾ oz cornflour

20 g/¾ oz plain flour

2 egg yolks

300 ml/10 fl oz milk

grated rind of 1 lime

300 ml/10 fl oz double cream

1 tsp vanilla extract

2 tbsp icing sugar

toasted coconut curls or desiccated coconut

An all-American favourite made with a coconut confectioners' custard and topped with vanilla cream. Ginger fans could try a little chopped crystallised stem ginger in the cream instead of the vanilla flavouring.

1. Preheat the oven to 180°C/350°F/Gas Mark 4. Lightly grease a 12-section muffin tin.

2. Put the syrup and butter in a small saucepan. Heat gently, uncovered, stirring, until the butter has just melted. Take the saucepan off the heat and stir in the biscuit crumbs. Divide the mixture between the sections of the prepared tin. Press it firmly over the base and sides of the tin with the back of a teaspoon.

3. Line the cases with baking paper and fill with baking beans, then bake them in the preheated oven for 8–10 minutes, or until slightly darker in colour. Leave to cool and harden in the tin for 10–15 minutes. Remove the paper and beans.

4. Put the coconut into a mixing bowl and pour over the boiling water. Leave to stand for 10 minutes. Put the sugar, cornflour, plain flour and egg yolks in a separate mixing bowl and beat together.

5. Pour the milk into a small saucepan, bring just to the boil, then gradually whisk it into the egg yolk mixture until smooth. Return the milk mixture to the saucepan and cook over a medium heat, whisking, until thick. The sauce will suddenly thicken, and as it does you may find it easier to turn the heat right down to low so that you can whisk out any lumps quickly. Stir in the soaked coconut and the lime rind, cover the surface with wetted baking paper and leave to cool.

6. Loosen the pie cases with a round-bladed knife and carefully lift out of the tin. Spoon in the coconut filling.

7. Whip the cream until it just forms soft swirls, then fold in the vanilla extract and sugar. Spoon this over the tops of the pies, then decorate with coconut curls or desiccated coconut.

Mini Desserts

Cooking techniques

Freezing

If you are freezing desserts served in glasses, choose plastic glasses. Arrange the desserts on a baking tray or in a plastic box and freeze them uncovered until firm, then cover with cling film or the plastic box lid, seal and label. Use within 6 weeks. Defrost desserts in the fridge overnight or at room temperature for 2 hours, then transfer to the fridge. If the desserts have been frozen, do not return any leftover desserts to the freezer.

Gelatine

To use powered gelatine, scoop the powder into a measuring teaspoon so it is level with the spoon, then sprinkle it over cold water in a small heatproof bowl. If specks remain on the surface of the water, gently stir them in using a teaspoon. Allow the gelatine to soak for 5 minutes (it forms a sponge-like mixture), then stand the bowl in a small saucepan and pour water into the pan halfway up the bowl. Gently simmer the water for 5 minutes, until the gelatine melts and is a clear, straw-coloured liquid. If it gets very hot, allow it to cool for a few minutes. Trickle the gelatine into your wine, juice or cream. Pour the mixture straight into serving dishes (if the jelly contains sliced fruit, which may float, allow the jelly to partially set before adding it to the serving dishes). Chill in the fridge for 3–4 hours.

To turn a jelly out, dip a metal mould into just-boiled water for 2 seconds (longer if it is silicone), then loosen the top of the jelly with your fingertips and invert the mould onto a serving plate. Holding the mould and plate, give a quick jerk, remove the mould and clean the dish with kitchen paper. Serve within 30 minutes.

Caramel

The secret to caramel is to avoid stirring the sugar as it dissolves, as this can make it crystallize. Heat the sugar and water gently in a heavy-based saucepan, tilting it from time to time. Once the sugar has dissolved, boil rapidly for 4–5 minutes; the syrup will colour around the edges and then will burn easily, so do not leave the pan unattended. Tilt the pan gently to encourage even colouring. When browned remove from the heat.

Meringues

Always use a clean, dry bowl and whisk. Whisk the egg whites until they form stiff, moist-looking peaks, then tilt the bowl; they won't move if they are ready. Gradually whisk in the sugar, a teaspoonful at a time, then continue to whisk for 1–2 minutes after it has been added to make the mixture smooth, thickened and glossy. Spoon or pipe onto baking trays lined with non-stick baking paper and bake in a low oven, as specified in the recipe, until the meringues are crisp and can be lifted easily off the paper. If they are sticky on the base, cook for a few minutes longer, then try again. Cooled unfilled meringues will keep in a cool place in a biscuit tin layered with baking paper for 3–4 days.

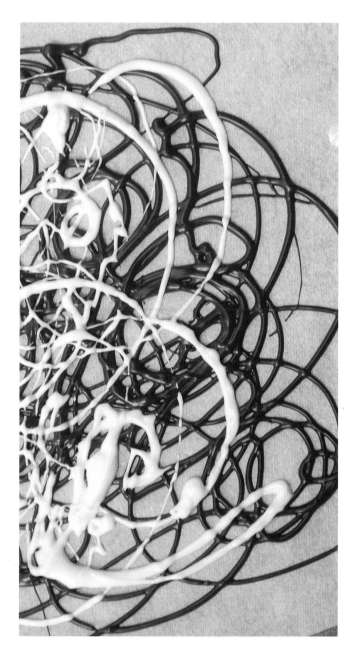

Decorating techniques

Chocolate curls

Spread just-melted chocolate over a marble pastry board or cheese board into a thin, even layer no less than 5 mm/¾ inch thick. Leave in a cool place to set. Draw a long cook's knife across the chocolate at a 45° angle in a see-saw action to shave the chocolate into curls. For two-tone chocolate caraque, spread a band of melted white chocolate on the marble, leave to set for 5 minutes, then spread a band of melted dark chocolate onto it, butting up to the white chocolate, making sure that the level of the chocolate is the same for both types. Leave to set, then shave into curls as above.

For speedy chocolate curls, turn a block of chocolate over so that the smooth underside is uppermost, then place the block on a chopping board and run a vegetable peeler firmly over the surface so that the blade is at a slight angle to the chocolate. The size of the curl that you make will depend on the temperature of the chocolate and the amount of fat it contains. If the chocolate is very cold, the curls will be tiny, so soften it in the microwave at full power for 10 seconds (if the bar is large or the chocolate is dark, you may need to give it a second burst in the microwave). The fewer cocoa solids the chocolate contains, the easier it will be to shape, so white and milk chocolate will make larger curls than plain chocolate.

Piped chocolate

Spoon melted chocolate into a small non-stick baking paper piping bag (see page 10), roll down the top to enclose the chocolate, then snip a little off the tip of the bag. There is no need to add a piping nozzle. Pipe shapes such as leaves, flowers, butterflies, initials and hearts over non-stick baking paper freehand, or draw them on a second sheet of paper using a black pen, then slide it under the top sheet before piping. Fill in the shapes with extra piped squiggles of chocolate or flood the centre to fill completely.

Coloured chocolate

Melted white chocolate can be coloured with the tiniest amount of liquid food colouring and can make an eye-catching decoration piped over a layer of dark chocolate.

Sugar decorations

Ready-to-roll fondant icing can be left white or coloured with paste or gel food colourings before being shaped. Don't use liquid food colourings, as these will make the icing sticky and tricky to roll out. Paste or gel colours can be bought from supermarkets, specialist cookshops or online in a wide variety of colours. Apply the colouring to the icing on the end of a cocktail stick and use sparingly. Knead the colouring in, then roll the icing out thinly and stamp out stars, holly leaves, snowflakes or tiny hearts or flowers using cutters. (Look out for mini-plunger flower cutters, as these can be depressed into a small circle of foam for a curved flower effect). Allow the decorations to dry at room temperature on a tray lined with non-stick baking paper, then store them in a small plastic box, interleaved with extra paper, for up to 2 months. You can also buy ready-made sugar flowers or choose from a range of edible glitter, sugar strands or tiny shapes from supermarkets or specialist suppliers.

Natural flower decorations

Tiny flowers from the garden can add a delicate finishing touch to a miniature dessert, but first make sure that they are edible. Choose from tiny viola or pansy flowers in a mix of colours to borage, violet, little rose petals or herb flowers or tiny mint leaves. Brush petals or leaves lightly with a little beaten egg white, then sprinkle with caster sugar and allow to dry on a tray lined with non-stick baking paper for an hour. Use immediately.

Citrus curls

Pare away the rind from lemons, oranges or limes with a zester (a small metal-topped tool with a row of holes punched in the top). Dust the curls with a little caster sugar and sprinkle them over mousses or ice creams. For larger, corkscrew-type curls, remove the citrus peel in single, slightly larger strips with a canelle knife, then twist each strip tightly around a cocktail stick, leave for a minute, slide the cocktail stick out and hang the corkscrew curl over the edge of the serving dish.

Caramel shards

Just-cooked caramel can be drizzled over non-stick baking paper, then left to cool and harden. When ready to serve, break it into shards or chop it into small pieces. Chopped or flaked nuts can also be added before it hardens, for extra interest.

Blueberry and maple syrup pancakes

Makes: 30
Prep: 20 minutes
Cook: 10–15 minutes

Popular with diners of all ages, these bite-sized pancakes take only a few minutes to prepare – which is just as well, as the chances are they will disappear as soon as they are cooked.

175 g/6 oz plain flour

1 tsp baking powder

½ tsp bicarbonate of soda

1 tbsp caster sugar

2 eggs, separated

finely grated rind of 1 lemon and juice of ½ lemon

250 ml/9 fl oz milk

115 g/4 oz blueberries

a little sunflower oil, for frying

maple syrup, to serve

crème fraîche, to serve (optional)

1. Put the flour, baking powder and bicarbonate of soda into a mixing bowl, then stir in the sugar. Whisk the egg whites in a separate large, clean mixing bowl until you have soft peaks.

2. Add the egg yolks, lemon rind and lemon juice to the flour, then gradually whisk in the milk until smooth. Fold in a spoonful of the whisked egg whites, then add the rest and fold in gently. Sprinkle the blueberries into the bowl, then gently and briefly fold them in.

3. Pour a little oil into a large frying pan, then place it over a medium heat. When it's hot, drop dessertspoonfuls of the blueberry mixture into the pan, leaving a little space between the pancakes. Cook for 2–3 minutes, until bubbles appear on the surface of the pancakes and the undersides are golden. Turn the pancakes over and cook the second side for 1–2 minutes, until golden.

4. Remove the pancakes from the pan using a palette knife and keep them hot in a clean tea towel. Cook the remaining blueberry mixture in batches of 10 pancakes at a time, until all the mixture is cooked, oiling the pan as needed.

5. Transfer the pancakes to small dessert plates, serving 4–5 pancakes per portion. Drizzle a little maple syrup over them and serve extra syrup in a small jug. Top the pancakes with teaspoonfuls of crème fraîche if liked.

Berry and oat crumbles

Makes: 8
Prep: 20 minutes
Cook: 20 minutes

These homely little puddings are always a great hit. If you wish, make double the amount of crumble topping and store it in the freezer, then use it at a later date and bake from frozen.

450 g/1 lb red plums, halved, stoned and diced

115 g/4 oz raspberries

25 g/1 oz light muscovado sugar

3 tbsp water

ready-made custard, to serve

TOPPING

85 g/3 oz plain flour

20 g/¾ oz porridge oats

20 g/¾ oz barley flakes

40 g/1½ oz light muscovado sugar

40 g/1½ oz unsalted butter, chilled and diced

1. Preheat the oven to 180°C/350°F/Gas Mark 4. Put the plums, raspberries, sugar and water into a heavy-based saucepan. Cover and simmer for 5 minutes, or until the fruit has softened.

2. For the topping, put the flour, porridge oats, barley flakes and sugar into a mixing bowl and stir. Rub in the butter using your fingertips until the mixture resembles fine crumbs.

3. Spoon the fruit mixture into 8 x 150-ml/5-fl oz metal pudding moulds and stand them on a baking tray. Sprinkle the topping on top.

4. Bake in the preheated oven for 15 minutes, or until golden. Allow the crumbles to cool for 5–10 minutes, then serve topped with small spoonfuls of custard.

Cinnamon and apple fritters with blackberry sauce

Makes: 30
Prep: 30 minutes
Cook: 20–35 minutes

A retro dessert that uses storecupboard ingredients. It's a good way to make the most of blackberries you have in the freezer. Alternatively, use whatever frozen berries you have to hand – raspberries or blackcurrants would work well.

8 small dessert apples

150 g/5½ oz blackberries

125 ml/4 fl oz water

6 tbsp caster sugar

150 g/5½ oz plain flour

a large pinch of ground cinnamon

1 egg, separated

150 ml/5 fl oz milk

1 litre/1¾ pints sunflower oil

1. For the sauce, quarter, core, peel and dice 2 of the apples, then put them into a heavy-based saucepan. Add the blackberries, water and 1 tablespoon of the sugar. Cover and simmer for 5–10 minutes, or until the apples have softened. Purée until smooth using a handheld blender, then press through a sieve into a serving bowl to remove the seeds. Cover with cling film and set aside.

2. Peel and core the remaining apples, cut them into thin rings, then put them in a plastic bag with 40 g/1½ oz of the flour. Seal the bag, then shake to coat the apples thinly with the flour.

3. Put the remaining flour into a mixing bowl. Stir in 1 tablespoon of the sugar, the cinnamon and the egg yolk. Gradually whisk in the milk until smooth.

4. Whisk the egg white in a separate large, clean mixing bowl until you have soft peaks. Fold it into the flour mixture.

5. Pour the oil into a saucepan, making sure that it is no more than half full. Heat to 160°C/325°F on a sugar thermometer, or until bubbles form when a little batter is dropped into the oil. Line a plate with kitchen paper.

6. Shake any excess flour from the apple slices, then dip them into the batter and remove them using 2 forks. Drain off the excess batter, then carefully add 4–5 apple slices to the hot oil and cook for 2–3 minutes, or until golden. Lift out of the oil with a draining spoon, then transfer to the lined plate and leave to drain while you cook the remaining apples in batches of this size.

7. Sprinkle the remaining sugar over the fritters and serve with the blackberry sauce for dipping.

Hot orange soufflés with chocolate and orange sauce

Makes: 12
Prep: 25 minutes
Cook: 20–25 minutes

Serving hot soufflés adds a touch of theatre to any meal as they puff up dramatically in the oven but fall just as quickly. Get your dinner guests ready and waiting, dust the tops of the soufflés with a speedy flourish of icing sugar, then serve, hopefully, to applause.

25 g/1 oz unsalted butter, for greasing

115 g/4 oz caster sugar, plus 2 tbsp for sprinkling

3 eggs, separated, plus 1 extra egg white

40 g/1½ oz plain flour

225 ml/8 fl oz milk

finely grated rind of 1 large orange

5 tbsp orange juice, or 3 tbsp orange juice plus 2 tbsp Cointreau

a large pinch of ground cinnamon

icing sugar, sifted, for dusting

SAUCE

150 g/5½ oz plain chocolate, roughly chopped

4 tbsp orange juice

2 tbsp caster sugar

1. Grease 12 x 125-ml/4-fl oz wide-topped ovenproof demitasse coffee cups with the butter, then sprinkle them with 2 tablespoons of caster sugar, tilting to coat them evenly. Put them on a baking tray and set aside.

2. Put half the measured sugar and all the egg yolks into a mixing bowl and beat together for 2 minutes using an electric handheld whisk, until thick and pale. Sift the flour over the surface, then fold it in.

3. Pour the milk into a medium heavy-based saucepan, bring just to the boil, then gradually whisk it into the egg mixture until smooth. Pour the mixture back into the pan, then cook over a low heat, whisking gently, until thickened and smooth.

4. Remove the soufflé mixture from the heat and whisk in the orange rind, juice, Cointreau if using, and cinnamon. Cover with cling film and leave to cool.

5. Preheat the oven to 190°C/375°F/Gas Mark 5. Whisk the egg whites in a large, clean mixing bowl until you have stiff, moist-looking peaks. Gradually whisk in the remaining sugar, a teaspoonful at a time. Fold the whites into the cooled soufflé mixture, then divide between the 12 dishes so that they are three-quarters full. Bake in the preheated oven for 15–20 minutes, or until the soufflés are well risen, the tops are golden and they are almost set in the centre.

6. Meanwhile, to make the sauce, put the chocolate, orange juice and sugar in a heatproof bowl, set the bowl over a saucepan of gently simmering water and heat until smooth and melted, stirring from time to time. Pour into a jug.

7. Quickly serve the soufflés on saucers, dust with sifted icing sugar and drizzle the warm chocolate sauce over the top.

Cranberry and granola sundaes

Makes: 10
Prep: 20 minutes
Cook: 13–15 minutes

With the mix of tangy, slightly sharp cranberry compote, creamy smooth Greek yogurt and crunchy granola, this is a great dessert or party brunch. Make up extra granola and serve in little dishes as an alternative to crisps.

a little sunflower oil, for greasing

2 tbsp sesame seeds

2 tbsp pumpkin seeds

25 g/1 oz porridge oats

25 g/1 oz flaked almonds

40 g/1½ oz unsalted butter

2 tbsp runny honey

2 tbsp light muscovado sugar

250 g/9 oz honey-flavoured Greek yogurt

CRANBERRY COMPOTE

2 tsp cornflour

85 g/3 oz light muscovado sugar

juice of 1 large orange

200 g/7 oz frozen cranberries

1. Preheat the oven to 180°C/350°F/Gas Mark 4. Lightly brush a large baking tray with oil.

2. Put the sesame seeds, pumpkin seeds, porridge oats and flaked almonds into a bowl and mix together using your fingertips. Put the butter, honey and sugar into a heavy-based saucepan and heat gently until the butter has melted and the sugar dissolved. Remove from the heat and stir in the seed mixture. Tip onto the prepared baking tray and spread into a thin, even layer. Bake in the preheated oven for 8–10 minutes, stirring halfway through cooking and moving the browned edges to the centre. Allow to cool in the tin.

3. For the cranberry compote, put the cornflour, sugar and orange juice into a heavy-based saucepan and cook over a medium heat, stirring, until smooth. Add the frozen cranberries and cook, uncovered, for 5 minutes, stirring, until they have softened and the juices have thickened. Allow to cool.

4. Crumble half the granola using your fingertips and break the rest into shards. Sprinkle a layer of the crumble into 10 shot glasses, spoon on a layer of yogurt, then a layer of cranberry compote. Repeat the layers, finishing with a layer of compote, and decorate with the shards of granola. Any remaining granola shards can be served in a small separate dish.

Chocolate fondants with toffee sauce

Makes: 10
Prep: 25 minutes
Chill: 1 hour or overnight
Cook: 17–20 minutes

This restaurant favourite is surprisingly easy to make and can be prepared in advance then left in the fridge for up to 24 hours. The secret is to bake the puddings for precisely the cooking time and test one before serving them. They should be crusty on top but soft and molten in the centre.

150 g/5½ oz unsalted butter

4 tsp cocoa powder

150 g/5½ oz plain chocolate, roughly chopped

2 eggs, plus 2 egg yolks

125 g/4½ oz caster sugar

25 g/1 oz plain flour

icing sugar, sifted, for dusting

TOFFEE SAUCE

55 g/2 oz unsalted butter

55 g/2 oz light muscovado sugar

1 tbsp runny honey

150 ml/5 fl oz double cream

1. Melt 25 g/1 oz of the butter in a small saucepan, then brush it over the insides of 10 x 125-ml/4-fl oz ovenproof ramekins. Sift a little cocoa into each ramekin, then tilt to coat the base and sides evenly, tapping out any excess.

2. Put the chocolate and remaining 125 g/4½ oz butter in a heatproof bowl, set the bowl over a saucepan of gently simmering water and heat until melted, stirring from time to time.

3. Put the eggs, egg yolks and caster sugar into a mixing bowl and whisk together until thick and frothy and the whisk leaves a trail when raised above the mixture. Sift over the flour, then gently fold it in.

4. Fold the melted chocolate mixture into the egg mixture until smooth. Pour it into the prepared ramekins, cover and chill in the fridge for 1 hour, or overnight if time allows.

5. For the toffee sauce, put the butter, light muscovado sugar and honey into a heavy-based saucepan and heat gently for 3–4 minutes, or until the butter has melted and the sugar dissolved, then boil for 1–2 minutes, stirring, until it begins to smell of toffee and thicken. Remove from the heat and stir in the cream.

6. Preheat the oven to 180°C/350°F/Gas Mark 4. Take the ramekins out of the fridge and leave at room temperature for 10 minutes. Bake in the preheated oven for 10–12 minutes, or until well risen, the tops are crusty and the centres still slightly soft. Reheat the sauce over a low heat, if needed.

7. Dust the desserts with sifted icing sugar. Serve immediately with the sauce in a jug for guests to pour on.

Raspberry and strawberry pavlovas

Makes: 20
Prep: 25 minutes
Cook: 25–30 minutes

Spoil the ones you love with these gorgeous-looking meringues. You can make them in advance and keep them in an airtight tin for several days, then just make the topping when you are ready to serve them.

2 egg whites

115 g/4 oz caster sugar

½ tsp cornflour

½ tsp white wine vinegar

TOPPING

300 ml/10 fl oz double cream

finely grated rind and juice of
1 lime

3 tbsp strawberry jam

200 g/7 oz raspberries

200 g/7 oz small strawberries,
hulled and sliced

1. Preheat the oven to 140°C/275°F/Gas Mark 1. Line a large baking tray with non-stick baking paper.

2. Whisk the egg whites in a large, clean mixing bowl until you have stiff, moist-looking peaks. Gradually whisk in the sugar a tablespoonful at a time. Once all the sugar has been added, whisk for a further 1–2 minutes, until the meringue is thick and glossy.

3. Mix the cornflour and vinegar together in a small bowl until smooth, then fold it into the meringue. Spoon the mixture onto the prepared baking tray in 20 mounds, leaving a little space between each mound. Spread it into circles 5 cm/2 inches in diameter, then make a small dip in the centre of each circle using the back of a teaspoon.

4. Bake in the preheated oven for 25–30 minutes, or until the meringues are a very pale biscuit colour and can easily be lifted off the paper. If they stick to the paper, cook them for a few minutes longer, then retest. Leave to cool on the paper.

5. For the topping, pour the cream into a large mixing bowl and whisk until it forms soft swirls, then fold in the lime rind. Spoon a dollop of the cream onto the top of each pavlova, then transfer to a serving plate.

6. Put the jam and lime juice in a small heavy-based saucepan and place over a gentle heat until the jam has just melted. Stir in the raspberries and strawberries, then leave to cool a little. Spoon the fruit over the pavlovas and serve.

Strawberry and rosé jellies

Makes: 8
Prep: 20 minutes
Cook: 5 minutes
Chill: 4 hours

A pretty finale to any summer celebration. If you have roses in the garden you may like to decorate the cream with tiny pink rose petals instead of finely grated lemon rind.

150 g/5½ oz small strawberries, hulled and sliced

1½ tbsp caster sugar

3 tbsp water

2 tsp powdered gelatine

200 ml/7 fl oz rosé wine

TOPPING

1½ tbsp caster sugar

2 tbsp rosé wine

finely grated rind of 1 lemon

150 ml/5 fl oz double cream

1. Put the strawberries and sugar into a mixing bowl and mix together using a metal spoon.

2. Put the water in a small heatproof bowl, then sprinkle the gelatine over the surface, making sure the powder is absorbed. Set aside for 5 minutes. Set the bowl of gelatine in a saucepan of gently simmering water and heat for about 5 minutes, stirring from time to time, until the gelatine is a clear liquid (see page 116).

3. Divide the sugar-coated strawberries between 8 small champagne or liqueur glasses. Pour the 200 ml/7 fl oz wine into a measuring jug and stir in the gelatine, then pour it into the glasses. Cover and chill in the fridge for 4 hours, or until the jelly has set.

4. To make the topping, put the sugar, wine and half the lemon rind into a small bowl and stir. Pour the cream into a large mixing bowl and whisk until it forms soft swirls. Add the wine mixture and whisk briefly, until the cream is thick again. Spoon the lemon cream into the centre of the jellies, then decorate with the remaining lemon rind.

Rippled raspberry cheesecakes

Makes: 12
Prep: 30 minutes
Cook: 5 minutes
Chill: 3 hours

55 g/2 oz unsalted butter

115 g/4 oz digestive biscuits,

crushed

3 tbsp water

2 tsp powdered gelatine

150 g/5½ oz raspberries, plus 24
to decorate

150 ml/5 fl oz double cream

150 ml/5 fl oz ready-made custard

¼ tsp vanilla extract

Silicone trays make turning out these dainty desserts child's play. The swirled effect is simple to create but looks really impressive.

1. Melt the butter in a saucepan, then stir in the biscuit crumbs. Divide the mixture between the sections of 2 x 6-section silicone muffin trays; the base of each cup should be 4 cm/1½ inches in diameter. Press over the base of the sections using the back of a teaspoon, then chill in the fridge.

2. Put the water in a small heatproof bowl, then sprinkle the gelatine over the surface, making sure the powder is absorbed. Set aside for 5 minutes. Meanwhile, purée the 150 g/5½ oz raspberries in a blender, then press through a sieve into a bowl to remove the seeds. Set the bowl of gelatine in a saucepan of gently simmering water and heat for about 5 minutes, stirring from time to time, until the gelatine is a clear liquid (see page 116).

3. Pour the cream into a large mixing bowl and whisk until it forms soft swirls. Fold in the custard and vanilla. Stir 1½ tablespoons of the gelatine into the raspberry purée and fold the rest into the cream mixture. Spoon the cream mixture into the muffin trays, level the surface using the back of a teaspoon, then spoon the raspberry purée on top. Swirl the two mixtures together using the handle of the teaspoon. Cover and chill in the fridge for 3 hours, or longer if time allows, until set.

4. To serve, loosen the desserts using a round-bladed knife, then turn them out by pressing underneath. Decorate each dessert with 2 raspberries.

Lemon and blueberry duets

Makes: 10
Prep: 15 minutes
Cook: 5 minutes
Chill: 1–2 hours

300 ml/10 fl oz double cream

90 g/3¼ oz caster sugar

finely grated rind and juice of
1 lemon, plus grated rind of
1 lemon to decorate

1 tsp cornflour

4 tbsp water

250 g/9 oz blueberries

If you need a pudding in a hurry, then this is it. It takes just 20 minutes to make, then can be left in the fridge to chill until you are ready to serve.

1. Put the cream and 75 g/2¾ oz sugar into a medium heavy-based saucepan, then heat gently, stirring, until the sugar has dissolved. Increase the heat and bring to the boil, then cook for 1 minute, stirring.

2. Remove from the heat, add half the finely grated lemon rind and all the juice, and stir continuously for 1 minute, until the mixture begins to thicken slightly. Pour into 10 shot glasses, then leave to cool.

3. Put the remaining sugar and finely grated lemon rind into a smaller heavy-based saucepan, stir in the cornflour, then gradually mix in the water until smooth. Add half the blueberries, then place over a medium heat and cook, stirring, for 3–4 minutes, until they are starting to soften and the sauce thicken.

4. Remove the compote from the heat, stir in the remaining blueberries, then leave to cool. Cover the glasses and blueberry compote with cling film, then transfer to the fridge for 1–2 hours, or until set.

5. When ready to serve, stir the blueberries, then spoon them into the glasses and decorate with the grated lemon rind.

White chocolate and strawberry cheesecakes

Makes: 40
Prep: 30 minutes
Cook: 45–50 minutes
Chill: overnight

An all-American favourite, this baked cheesecake tastes even better the day after it is made.

SPONGE

55 g/2 oz margarine, softened

55 g/2 oz caster sugar

55 g/2 oz self-raising flour

1 egg

CHEESECAKE

200 g/7 oz white chocolate, roughly chopped

600 g/1lb 5 oz full-fat soft cheese

85 g/3 oz caster sugar

1 tsp vanilla extract

200 ml/7 fl oz double cream

4 eggs

TOPPING

250 ml/9 fl oz crème fraîche

10 strawberries, hulled and quartered

55 g/2 oz white chocolate, cut into shards using a swivel vegetable peeler

1. Preheat the oven to 180°C/350°F/Gas Mark 4. Line a 30 x 20 x 5-cm/12 x 8 x 2-inch loose-bottomed cake tin with non-stick baking paper, snipping diagonally into the corners, then pressing the paper into the tin so that the base and sides are lined.

2. Put all the sponge ingredients into a mixing bowl and beat together using a wooden spoon until smooth. Spoon the mixture into the prepared tin and spread it into a thin layer using a spatula. Bake in the preheated oven for 10–12 minutes, or until golden and firm to the touch. Remove from the oven and leave to cool. Reduce the oven temperature to 150°C/300°F/Gas Mark 2.

3. For the cheesecake, put the chocolate in a heatproof bowl, set the bowl over a saucepan of gently simmering water and heat until melted. Stir briefly and leave to cool. Meanwhile, put the soft cheese, sugar and vanilla extract into a mixing bowl and beat together briefly using an electric handheld whisk until just smooth. Gradually beat in the cream until thick once more. Beat in the eggs one at a time, waiting until the mixture is smooth before adding the next one. Stir in the melted chocolate.

4. Spoon the cheesecake mixture onto the sponge and spread it out so it forms an even layer. Bake in the preheated oven for 30–35 minutes, or until the edge is slightly cracked and the centre still a little soft. Turn off the oven, leave the door ajar and leave to cool.

5. Cover the cheesecake and put it in the fridge overnight. When ready to serve, remove the cheesecake from the tin, peel off the baking paper and cut into 40 squares. Put these on a serving plate and top each square with a spoonful of crème fraîche. Add a quarter of a strawberry to each square and sprinkle with white chocolate shards.

Apricot and chocolate meringues

Makes: 12
Prep: 20 minutes
Cook: 10–13 minutes

Quick and easy to make, these pretty puddings look lovely served on a plate or platter. When apricots are out of season, try making these with halved plums.

6 apricots, halved and stoned

juice of ½ small orange

1 egg white

2 tbsp caster sugar

40 g/1½ oz plain chocolate, cut into 12 pieces

1. Preheat the oven to 180°C/350°F/Gas Mark 4.

2. Arrange the apricots, cut side up, on a baking tray. Drizzle the orange juice over the top of them. Bake in the preheated oven for 5–8 minutes.

3. Meanwhile, whisk the egg white in a large, clean mixing bowl until you have stiff, moist-looking peaks. Gradually whisk in the sugar a teaspoonful at a time. Once all the sugar has been added, whisk for a further 1–2 minutes, until the meringue is thick and glossy.

4. Spoon the meringue into a piping bag fitted with a medium star nozzle. Put a piece of chocolate in the centre of each apricot.

5. If the apricots wobble, stick them to the baking tray with a little meringue. Pipe a whirl of meringue on top of the chocolate. Bake in the preheated oven for 5 minutes, or until the meringue is tinged golden brown and just cooked. Allow to cool for a few minutes, then transfer to a serving plate.

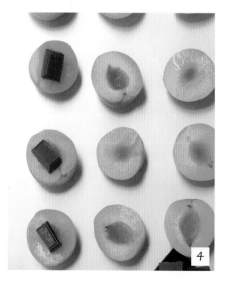

Baby blueberry brûlées

Makes: 12
Prep: 20 minutes
Cook: 15 minutes
Chill: 3-4 hours

This is a girlie pudding, in health-conscious-sized portions – although it will be hard to resist the temptation of second helpings!

125 g/4½ oz blueberries

4 egg yolks

1 tsp vanilla extract

100 g/3½ oz caster sugar

300 ml/10 fl oz double cream

1. Preheat the oven to 160°C/325°F/Gas Mark 3. Put 12 x 50-ml/2-fl oz ovenproof dishes in a large roasting tin and divide the blueberries between them.

2. Put the egg yolks, vanilla and 40 g/1½ oz sugar into a jug and mix together using a fork until smooth and creamy. Pour the cream into a small heavy-based saucepan, bring to the boil, then gradually mix it into the yolks. Strain the mixture through a sieve back into the pan before pouring it back into the jug.

3. Pour the cream mixture over the blueberries. Pour warm water into the roasting tin to come halfway up the sides of the dishes. Bake in the preheated oven for 15 minutes, or until the custard is just set, with a slight wobble in the centre.

4. Allow to cool for 5–10 minutes, then lift the dishes out of the water and transfer to the fridge to chill for 3–4 hours.

5. To serve, sprinkle the remaining sugar over the dishes in an even layer, then caramelize it using a cook's blow torch or under a grill preheated to hot.

Berry torte

Makes: 20
Prep: 40 minutes
Cook: 25–30 minutes

Spoil the ones you love with these dainty, rich, dark-chocolate cakes layered with minty strawberries and swirled with rich chocolate cream. If you don't have a heart-shaped biscuit cutter, use a small round one instead.

85 g/3 oz cocoa powder

250 ml/9 fl oz boiling water

115 g/4 oz unsalted butter, softened

250 g/9 oz light muscovado sugar

2 eggs, beaten

200 g/7 oz plain flour

1 tsp baking powder

FILLING

150 ml/5 fl oz double cream

115 g/4 oz strawberries, hulled and finely chopped

1 tbsp finely chopped fresh mint

1 tbsp caster sugar

FROSTING

150 ml/5 fl oz double cream

150 g/5½ oz plain chocolate, roughly chopped

1. Preheat the oven to 180°C/350°F/Gas Mark 4. Line a deep 25-cm/10-inch square loose-bottomed cake tin with non-stick baking paper, snipping diagonally into the corners, then pressing the paper into the tin so that the base and sides are lined.

2. Put the cocoa in a heatproof bowl, then gradually stir in the boiling water until you have a smooth paste. Leave to cool.

3. Put the butter and light muscovado sugar into a mixing bowl and beat together using an electric handheld whisk until light and fluffy. Gradually beat in the eggs and a tablespoon of flour, until smooth. Sift the remaining flour and the baking powder into the bowl and fold them in, then gradually stir in the cooled cocoa mixture.

4. Pour the mixture into the prepared cake tin and spread into an even layer using a spatula. Bake in the preheated oven for 25–30 minutes, or until risen and firm to the touch and a skewer inserted into the centre of the cake comes out clean. Leave to cool for 10 minutes, then transfer to a wire rack and leave to cool completely.

5. Remove the baking paper and, using a 5-cm/2-inch heart-shaped cutter, cut out 20 cakes. Cut each cake in half horizontally.

6. For the filling, pour the cream into a large mixing bowl and whisk until it forms soft swirls. Fold in the strawberries, mint and caster sugar, then spread the mixture over the bottom half of each cake and top with the other cake half. Put the cakes on a wire rack.

7. For the frosting, pour the cream into a small heavy-based saucepan and bring just to the boil. Remove from the heat and add the chocolate. Set aside for 5 minutes, then stir until smooth and glossy. Allow to cool for a further 15 minutes, until thick, then spoon onto, and spread over, the top of the cakes. Leave to set, then transfer to a serving plate.

Strawberry and mint ice cream cones

Makes: 24
Prep: 40 minutes
Cook: 15–20 minutes
Freeze: 6 hours 20 minutes

These pretty cones would be fun to serve at a family summer party. Keep a few in the freezer for a very special dollies' tea party to thrill any little girl and her friends.

CONES

55 g/2 oz unsalted butter

2 egg whites

115 g/4 oz caster sugar

a few drops of vanilla extract

55 g/2 oz plain flour

ICE CREAM

115 g/4 oz caster sugar

6 tbsp water

2 sprigs of mint

450 g/1 lb strawberries, hulled and sliced, plus extra to serve

3 tsp powdered gelatine

150 ml/5 fl oz double cream

1. Preheat the oven to 180°C/350°F/Gas Mark 4. Line 3 baking trays with non-stick baking paper. You will need 8 metal cream horn tins or homemade cones made out of cardboard covered with baking paper to use as moulds.

2. For the cones, melt the butter in a saucepan. Lightly whisk the egg whites in a large, clean mixing bowl until frothy but still translucent. Whisk in the sugar, then the melted butter and the vanilla. Sift in the flour, then fold it in until smooth. Drop 4–5 half-teaspoonfuls of the mixture over one of the prepared baking trays and spread each into a circle 5–6 cm/2–2½ inches in diameter. Bake in the preheated oven for 3–5 minutes, or until just golden at the edges.

3. Allow the baked biscuits to harden for a few moments, then loosen with a palette knife and quickly shape into small cones around the moulds. Leave to set for 1–2 minutes, then remove the moulds. Repeat baking and shaping cones until all the mixture is used up, then leave to cool. Don't bake too many biscuits at once, or they will harden before you can shape them.

4. For the ice cream, put the sugar, 2 tablespoons of water and the mint into a medium heavy-based saucepan. Heat gently, stirring from time to time, until the sugar has dissolved. Add the sliced strawberries, increase the heat slightly and cook for 3 minutes. Discard the mint, then purée the mixture in a blender until smooth. Press the purée through a sieve into a metal loaf tin.

5. Put the remaining water in a small heatproof bowl, then sprinkle the gelatine over the surface, making sure the powder is absorbed. Set aside for 5 minutes. Set the bowl of gelatine in a saucepan of gently simmering water and heat for about 5 minutes, stirring from time to time, until the gelatine is a clear liquid (see page 116). Gently stir the gelatine into the puréed strawberry mixture, leave to cool, then freeze for 20 minutes.

6. Pour the cream in a large mixing bowl and whisk until it forms soft swirls. Transfer the just-setting strawberry mixture to another large mixing bowl and whisk for a few minutes. Fold the cream into the strawberries. Stand the cones in small cups and pipe the ice cream into them. Freeze for 6 hours or overnight. To serve, arrange the cones in a glass bowl with extra strawberries.

Triple chocolate mousses

Makes: 36
Prep: 45 minutes
Cook: 2 minutes
Chill: overnight
Freeze: 45 minutes

These smart-looking desserts can be prepared the day before you plan to serve them, or even frozen, and are easier to slice if not fully defrosted.

55 g/2 oz unsalted butter

1 tbsp cocoa powder

150 g/5½ oz digestive biscuits, crushed

milk chocolate curls, to decorate

MOUSSE

4 tbsp water

4 tsp powdered gelatine

115 g/4 oz plain chocolate, roughly chopped

115 g/4 oz milk chocolate, roughly chopped

115 g/4 oz white chocolate, roughly chopped

125 g/4½ oz unsalted butter

6 tbsp milk

6 eggs, separated

½ tsp vanilla extract

350 ml/12 fl oz double cream

1. Line a deep 20-cm/8-inch square loose-bottomed cake tin with 2 long strips of cling film, laid over each other in a cross, then press into the tin. The edges of the cling film should hang over the sides of the tin.

2. Melt the butter in a small saucepan, then stir in the cocoa and biscuit crumbs. Press the mixture into the tin in an even layer, then cover and chill in the fridge.

3. For the mousse, put the water in a small heatproof bowl, then sprinkle the gelatine over the surface, making sure the powder is absorbed. Set aside for 5 minutes. Set the bowl of gelatine in a saucepan of gently simmering water and heat for 5 mintes, stirring from time to time, until the gelatine is a clear liquid (see page 116).

4. Put each type of chopped chocolate in a different heatproof bowl, then add one third of the butter and 2 tablespoons of milk to each bowl. Place each bowl over a saucepan of gently simmering water and heat until the chocolate has melted. Stir 2 egg yolks into each bowl one at a time then remove from the heat.

5. Stir 4 teaspoons of the dissolved gelatine into each bowl, then stir the vanilla into the white chocolate. Pour the cream into a fourth bowl and whisk until it forms soft swirls. Fold one third of the cream into each of the chocolate mixtures. Whisk the egg whites in a large, clean mixing bowl until you have soft peaks, then divide them between the chocolate bowls and fold in gently.

6. Pour the plain chocolate mousse into the biscuit-lined tin, spread it into an even layer, then freeze for 15 minutes. Spoon over the white chocolate layer and freeze for 30 minutes. Gently whisk the milk chocolate layer to soften, if needed, then spoon it over and chill in the fridge overnight, or until set.

7. To serve, lift the mousse out of the tin, pressing from the base. Peel off the cling film. Cut the mousse into 6 strips using a wet knife, then cut each strip into 6 small squares, wiping and wetting the knife frequently so that the layers don't become smeared. Arrange on small plates or saucers and decorate with milk chocolate curls.

Mini clementine granitas

Makes: 10
Prep: 25 minutes
Cook: 5 minutes
Freeze: 4 hours plus overnight

If you are serving these only to adults you might like to add a splash of Cointreau or Grand Marnier to the mixture before freezing.

10 clementines

85 g/3 oz granulated sugar

4 tbsp water

finely grated rind and juice of 1 lemon

juice of 1 large orange

1. Cut a thin slice off the top of each clementine and set aside. Squeeze a little of the juice from each fruit into a blender. Using a teaspoon, scoop the flesh into the blender, then whizz to a purée.

2. Press the purée through a sieve into a large loaf tin. Put the 10 clementine cups into a roasting tin and freeze.

3. Put the sugar and water into a heavy-based saucepan. Heat gently for 5 minutes, or until the sugar has dissolved, tilting the pan to mix them together. Increase the heat and boil rapidly, without stirring, for 1 minute. Remove from the heat, then stir in the lemon rind and juice. Pour the lemon syrup and orange juice onto the clementine purée through a sieve and stir, then leave to cool.

4. Transfer the loaf tin to the freezer and freeze for 2 hours, or until the mixture is semi-frozen. Break up the ice crystals using a fork, then return to the freezer for 1 hour. Beat again with the fork, then freeze for 1 more hour. Beat again until it resembles coloured snow.

5. Spoon the granita into the clementine cups, add the lids at a jaunty angle and freeze overnight. (If the granita has frozen too firmly, allow it to soften at room temperature for a few minutes, then beat with a fork.) When ready to serve, transfer the iced desserts to a plate.

Striped cranberry and amaretti creams

Makes: 10
Prep: 30 minutes
Cook: 5–8 minutes
Chill: 1 hour

An easy festive dessert that makes a great alternative to the traditional Christmas pudding. Children will love to help you make the sugar stars.

85 g/3oz caster sugar

2 tsp cornflour

a large pinch of ground cinnamon

a large pinch of ground ginger

125 ml/4 fl oz water

200 g/7 oz frozen cranberries

AMARETTI CREAM

150 g/5½ oz full-fat soft cheese

3 tbsp caster sugar

200 ml/7 fl oz double cream

4 tsp orange juice or Cointreau

55 g/2 oz amaretti biscuits, crushed

SUGAR STARS

icing sugar, for dusting

150 g/5½ oz ready-to-roll fondant icing

1. Put the sugar, cornflour, cinnamon and ginger into a medium heavy-based saucepan, then gradually mix in the water until smooth. Add the frozen cranberries and cook gently for 5–8 minutes, stirring from time to time, until they are soft and the compote has thickened. Cover and leave to cool.

2. For the amaretti cream, put the soft cheese and sugar into a mixing bowl and stir, then gradually whisk in the cream until smooth. Stir in the orange juice and then the biscuit crumbs. Spoon the mixture into a paper or plastic disposable piping bag. Spoon the cranberry compote into another disposable piping bag. Snip off the tips.

3. Pipe the amaretti cream into 10 shot glasses until they are one-quarter full. Pipe over half the cranberry compote, then repeat the layers. Cover and chill in the fridge while you make the sugar stars.

4. For the sugar stars, line a baking tray with non-stick baking paper. Lightly dust a work surface with icing sugar. Knead the icing lightly, then roll it out thinly. Stamp out stars of different sizes using tiny star cutters, then transfer to the prepared baking tray and leave to harden at room temperature for 1 hour, or until needed. Arrange the stars on the desserts and around the bases of the glasses just before you serve them.

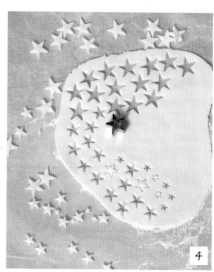

Chocolate and caramel cups

Makes: 12
Prep: 30 minutes
Cook: 7–8 minutes
Chill: 2 hours

If you don't have any petit four cases, line the sections of a mini muffin tin with small squares of cling film, spread melted chocolate over the cling film, then peel it away before serving.

150 g/5½ oz plain chocolate, roughly chopped

115 g/4 oz granulated sugar

4 tbsp water

12 small walnut halves

25 g/1 oz unsalted butter

125 ml/4 fl oz double cream

1. Line a 12-section mini muffin tin with paper petit four cases. Line a baking tray with non-stick baking paper.

2. Put the chocolate in a heatproof bowl, set the bowl over a saucepan of gently simmering water and heat until melted. Put a spoonful of melted chocolate into each paper case, then brush over the sides evenly using a small pastry brush. Chill for 30 minutes, then brush on a second layer of chocolate, taking care over the sides so there is an even thickness. Cover and chill in the fridge.

3. Put the sugar and water into a small heavy-based saucepan. Heat gently for 5 minutes, or until the sugar has dissolved, tilting the pan to mix them together. Increase the heat and boil rapidly without stirring for 4–5 minutes, until the caramel is deep golden (see page 116). Remove from the heat, add the walnuts, quickly coat them in the caramel, then lift them out using 2 forks. Put them on the prepared baking tray, slightly apart.

4. Add the butter to the remaining caramel, tilt the pan to mix, then gradually stir in the cream. Transfer to a bowl, leave to cool, then cover and chill in the fridge for 1½ hours, or until thick. Lift the chocolate-lined paper cases out of the tin. Spoon the caramel cream into a large piping bag fitted with a large star nozzle and pipe it into the chocolate cups. Chill in the fridge until required. Decorate with the caramel walnuts just before serving.

Cherry and honey terrines

Makes: 30
Prep: 25 minutes
Cook: 10 minutes
Freeze: 30 minutes
Chill: 5 hours

This two-tone dessert is made by setting the jelly mould at an angle before adding the creamy layer for an eye-catching effect.

300 g/10½ oz frozen stoned cherries

2 tbsp caster sugar

175 ml/6 fl oz water

4 tsp powdered gelatine

250 g/9 oz fromage frais

finely grated rind of 1 lemon

3 tbsp runny honey

150 ml/5 fl oz double cream

1. Put the frozen cherries, sugar and 125 ml/4 fl oz water into a medium heavy-based saucepan, bring to the boil, then reduce the heat and simmer, uncovered, for 5 minutes, until the cherries have softened.

2. Meanwhile, put the remaining water in a small heatproof bowl, then sprinkle the gelatine over the surface, making sure the powder is absorbed. Set aside for 5 minutes. Set the bowl of gelatine in a heavy-based saucepan of gently simmering water and heat for 5 minutes, stirring from time to time, until the gelatine is a clear liquid (see page 116).

3. Whizz the cherry mixture in a blender until puréed, then pour back into the heavy-based saucepan. Stir in 2½ tablespoons of the gelatine mixture, then leave to cool.

4. Divide the cherry mixture between 6 x 150-ml/5-fl oz loaf tins, prop them up in the freezer so that the jelly sets at an angle, then freeze for 30 minutes, or until firm.

5. Meanwhile, put the fromage frais, lemon rind and honey into a mixing bowl and stir together. Pour the cream into a large mixing bowl and whisk until it forms soft swirls, then fold it into the fromage frais mixture. Add the remaining gelatine mixture and stir gently, then cover and leave at room temperature.

6. When the semi-frozen jellies are ready, spoon the fromage frais over the top, level, then cover and chill in the fridge for 4 hours, or until set.

7. To turn out, dip each mould in a dish of just-boiled water for 2 seconds, then lift it out of the water. Loosen the edges of each dessert with a round-bladed knife, then turn out onto a plate, remove the tin and clean up the edge of the jelly with a sharp knife if needed. Return to the fridge for 1 hour, then slice each terrine into 5 and serve.

Honey and pistachio ice cream with poached figs

Makes: 10
Prep: 30–35 minutes
Cook: 10 minutes
Freeze: 1–7 hours

Refreshingly cool and summery, this Greek-inspired dessert can be made in advance and looks best served with small figs.

ICE CREAM

6 egg yolks

2 tsp cornflour

6 tbsp runny honey

450 ml/16 fl oz milk

250 g/9 oz Greek yogurt

2 tsp rosewater (optional)

55 g/2 oz pistachio nuts, roughly chopped

POACHED FIGS

150 ml/5 fl oz red wine

55 g/2 oz caster sugar

1 cinnamon stick, halved

10 small figs

1. For the ice cream, put the egg yolks, cornflour and honey into a large mixing bowl. Put the milk into a medium heavy-based saucepan, bring to the boil, then gradually whisk it into the yolks. Strain the mixture through a sieve back into the pan and cook over a low heat, stirring, until thickened and smooth. Pour the custard into a clean bowl, cover the surface with baking paper and leave to cool.

2. Whisk the yogurt and rosewater, if using, into the custard. Pour the mixture into a chilled ice cream machine and churn for 15–20 minutes, until thick and creamy. Mix in the pistachio nuts and churn until stiff enough to scoop. If you don't have an ice cream machine, pour into a large non-stick loaf tin for 3–4 hours, until semi-frozen. Beat in a food processor, then stir in the pistachio nuts, return to the loaf tin and freeze for a further 3 hours, or until firm.

3. Meanwhile, for the poached figs, put the wine, sugar and cinnamon stick into a small heavy-based saucepan and heat gently. Add the figs (they should fit snugly into the pan) and poach gently for 5 minutes. Leave to cool.

4. When ready to serve, take the ice cream out of the freezer and allow it to soften at room temperature for 5–10 minutes. Scoop into small dishes and add 2 fig halves and a little of the syrup. Serve immediately.

Blueberry vodka jellies

Makes: 12
Prep: 15 minutes
Cook: 8 minutes
Chill: 4 hours

This pretty dessert can be prepared in minutes. It looks stylish served in glasses of different heights then arranged on individual dessert plates or saucers and scattered with pink edible glitter.

6 trifle sponges or thin slices of shop-bought Madeira cake

350 ml/12 fl oz water

3 tsp powdered gelatine

250 g/9 oz blueberries

70 g/2½ oz caster sugar

finely grated rind of 1 lemon

100 ml/3½ fl oz vodka

125 ml/4 fl oz double cream

pink edible glitter, to decorate

1. Cut out 12 small circles of sponge, using the top of a liqueur glass as a guide, then press each of them into the base of a liqueur glass.

2. Put 50 ml/2 fl oz water into a small bowl, then sprinkle the gelatine over the surface, making sure the powder is absorbed. Set aside for 5 minutes.

3. Meanwhile, put the blueberries, sugar, lemon rind and remaining 300 ml/10 fl oz water into a heavy-based saucepan and bring to the boil, then reduce the heat and simmer, uncovered, for 5 minutes, until the fruit has softened.

4. Take the pan off the heat, add the gelatine and stir until it has dissolved. Add the vodka, then pour the mixture into the glasses, pressing down the sponge circles with a teaspoon if they begin to float. Leave to cool, then cover and put the glasses on a small baking tray. Chill in the fridge for 4 hours, or until set.

5. When ready to serve, spoon 2 teaspoons of the cream over the top of each dessert, then sprinkle with pink edible glitter.

Iced chocolate and peppermint mousses

Makes: 12
Prep: 40 minutes
Cook: 10 minutes
Freeze: 4 hours

A classic French dessert with a twist. As these little mousses are frozen, they can be made well in advance of your party. The drizzled chocolate decoration can be prepared the night before and left in the fridge until you are ready to serve.

150 g/5½ oz plain chocolate, roughly chopped

15 g/½ oz unsalted butter, diced

3 eggs, separated

2 tbsp milk

1 tbsp caster sugar

½ tsp peppermint extract

DECORATION

55 g/2 oz plain chocolate, roughly chopped

55 g/2 oz white chocolate, roughly chopped

a few drops of green food colouring

125 ml/4 fl oz double cream

½–1 tsp peppermint extract

1. For the mousse, put the plain chocolate and butter in a heatproof bowl, set the bowl over a saucepan of gently simmering water and heat until melted. Stir in the egg yolks, one at a time, then stir in the milk until smooth. Remove from the heat.

2. Whisk the egg whites in a large, clean mixing bowl until you have soft peaks. Gradually whisk in the sugar a teaspoonful at a time. Fold the egg whites into the melted chocolate mixture, then fold in the peppermint.

3. Spoon the mousse into 12 plastic shot glasses (if you have a funnel or large piping nozzle, spoon the mousse into this and pipe it into the glasses so that the sides don't get messy). Freeze for 4 hours, or overnight.

4. Meanwhile, for the decoration, line a baking tray with non-stick baking paper. Put the plain chocolate in a heatproof bowl, set the bowl over a heavy-based saucepan of gently simmering water and heat until melted. Drizzle spoonfuls of the melted chocolate over the prepared baking tray in random squiggles, then chill in the fridge for 30 minutes.

5. Put the white chocolate for the decoration in a heatproof bowl, set the bowl over a heavy-based saucepan of gently simmering water and heat until melted. Drizzle half the melted white chocolate over the plain chocolate on the baking tray. Stir the green food colouring into the remaining white chocolate and drizzle this over the other 2 layers of chocolate. Chill in the fridge for 30 minutes.

6. To decorate the mousses, pour the cream into a large bowl and whisk until it forms soft swirls, then stir in the peppermint extract. Spoon this onto the frozen desserts, then break the drizzled chocolate into pieces and press it into the cream. Allow the desserts to stand at room temperature for 10 minutes, then serve.

Tropical caramel custards

Makes: 10
Prep: 25 minutes
Cook: 30–35 minutes
Chill: 4 hours

A favourite dessert gets an exotic twist, with the addition of orange, lime and mango. If you don't have small metal pudding moulds, use little foil muffin or tart cases, but make sure they're 4 cm / 1½ inches deep.

175 g/6 oz granulated sugar

175 ml/6 fl oz water

3 tbsp boiling water

2 eggs, plus 2 egg yolks

150 ml/5 fl oz semi-skimmed milk

400 g/14 oz can sweetened full-fat condensed milk

finely grated rind of 1 orange

finely grated rind of 1 lime

½ small mango, peeled and stoned, to decorate

1. Preheat the oven to 160°C/325°F/Gas Mark 3. Put 10 x 150-ml/5-fl oz metal pudding or dariole moulds in a roasting tin.

2. Put the sugar and water into a heavy-based saucepan. Heat gently for 5 minutes, or until the sugar has dissolved, tilting the pan to mix them together. Increase the heat and boil rapidly without stirring for 5 minutes, until the caramel is deep golden (see page 116). Remove from the heat and add the boiling water, but stand well back as the syrup will spit. Allow the syrup to cool for 1 minute, or until the bubbles begin to subside, then divide it between the moulds.

3. Put the eggs and egg yolks into a large jug, then whisk lightly with a fork.

4. Pour the milk and condensed milk into a heavy-based saucepan. Bring just to the boil over a low heat, stirring constantly. Slowly pour this into the egg yolks, then strain back into the pan. Stir in the orange rind and half the lime rind (wrap the rest in cling film and reserve).

5. Pour the custard into the moulds. Pour warm water into the roasting tin to come halfway up the sides of the moulds. Bake in the preheated oven for 20–25 minutes, or until the custard is set. Lift the moulds out of the water, allow to cool, then chill in the fridge for 4 hours, or overnight.

6. To serve, cut the mango into small, thin slices. Dip each mould in a dish of just-boiled water for 10 seconds, then lift it out of the water. Loosen the edges of each dessert with a round-bladed knife, then invert them onto a plate and remove the mould. Serve topped with the mango slices and sprinkled with the reserved lime rind.

Mini Sweets

Equipment

Heavy-based saucepans

Good heavy-based saucepans in various sizes are crucial for working with sugar and chocolate, so they don't burn on the bottom of the pan.

Baking trays and tins

You'll need non-stick baking trays of various sizes, including 30 x 20 cm/12 x 8 inches, 28 x 18 cm/ 11 x 7 inches and 20 cm/8 inches square ones.

You'll also need a square loose-bottomed cake tin measuring 20 cm/8 inches and another measuring 17 cm/7 inches, as well as a heavy 20-cm/8-inch square baking tin and a 24-cm/10-inch square baking tin for fudge.

Be sure to buy good quality baking trays and tins – it really is worth it as they last a lifetime if they are well looked after.

Non-stick baking paper

Non-stick baking paper is invaluable for lining baking trays and tins.

Sugar thermometer

A sugar thermometer is essential for cooking sugar mixtures to a particular desired temperature. It will read between 37.7°C/100°F and 204.5°C/400°F in two-degree increments.

Make sure that the thermometer takes the temperature of the mixture in the pan and not of the bottom of the pan to get an accurate reading.

Electric mixer

The electric stand mixer is one of the most important tools for making sweets. It allows you to be hands-free while adding different ingredients or attending to other tasks as your ingredients are mixing.

Electric handheld whisk

The electric handheld whisk is crucial for whisking, blending and mixing ingredients for specific tasks, such as making macaroons.

Food Processor

The food processor is one of the most useful tools in the kitchen. It's terrific for chopping and grinding nuts as well as for blending mixtures.

Digital scales and measuring cups

It is essential to have digital scales, measuring cups and a set of measuring spoons.

Microplane Graters

Invest in stainless steel, razor-sharp graters in various sizes for different tasks, such as finely grating lemon rind and making chocolate curls.

Spatula

A heat-resistant spatula is invaluable for stirring mixtures as they cook.

Kitchen timer

Kitchen timers come in all shapes and sizes. Use a timer that is easy to read. Always set the timer for the least amount of time called for in the recipe – you can add more time if needed.

Cooking techniques

Melting chocolate

Put roughly chopped or broken chocolate in a sturdy heatproof bowl that will fit snugly over a heavy-based saucepan, so that no heat or steam can escape. Bring the saucepan of water to a gentle simmer, then set the bowl over it and continue simmering over a low heat until the chocolate has melted. Keep the water level in the pan at no more than 2.5 cm/1 inch deep and do not allow the bottom of the bowl containing the chocolate to touch the water or you may burn the chocolate. Once the chocolate has melted, use a rubber spatula to mix it until it is smooth. If you prefer to melt chocolate in a microwave, put the broken chocolate in a microwave-proof bowl and melt it on the lowest power in 30-second bursts. Stir with a rubber spatula after each burst.

Whisking eggs and egg whites

To whisk eggs to their full volume, it is best to have them at room temperature first. Use an electric stand mixer or handheld electric whisk with a bowl that is large enough for the eggs to triple in volume. Start with a medium speed and step it up to medium–high as the eggs increase in size. When whisking egg whites, it is very important that the bowl is clean with no trace of grease or fat, or they won't whisk properly. Egg whites can be frozen for up to 3 months. To defrost, allow them to come to room temperature before using.

Whisking cream

Chilled cream whisks best, as it holds onto the air whipped into it better. Chill the bowl and beaters if you can before whisking the cream. Start whisking on a medium speed and watch carefully as it can easily be over-whisked and get too firm. If this happens, you can rectify it by adding another couple of tablespoons of cream and whisking gently until it becomes smooth.

Chopping nuts

Chop nuts on a chopping board using a chef's knife, or pulse them using a food processor.

Strawberry ripple marshmallows

Makes: 32
Prep: 40 minutes
Cook: 20 minutes
Set: 1 hour

Light and fluffy, these pretty cubes of sweetness and light will put a smile on everyone's face. They are equally good made with raspberry extract instead of strawberry.

a little sunflower oil, for greasing

cornflour, for dusting

icing sugar, sifted, for dusting

11 sheets of leaf gelatine
(approximately 20 g/¾ oz)

340 ml/11½ fl oz water

1 tbsp liquid glucose

450 g/1 lb caster sugar

3 egg whites

1 tsp strawberry extract

2 tsp pink food colouring

1. Lightly brush a 30 x 20-cm/12 x 8-inch baking tray with oil, then lightly dust it with cornflour and sifted icing sugar.

2. Put the gelatine into a small bowl and add 140 ml/4½ fl oz water, making sure the gelatine is absorbed (see page 116). Set aside for 10 minutes.

3. Put the glucose, sugar and remaining 200 ml/7 fl oz water into a medium heavy-based saucepan. Bring to the boil, then reduce the heat and simmer for 15 minutes, or until the mixture reaches 127°C/260°F on a sugar thermometer. Remove from the heat, stir the gelatine mixture, then carefully spoon it into the pan; the syrup will bubble up. Pour the syrup into a measuring jug and stir.

4. Whisk the egg whites in a large, clean mixing bowl until you have stiff, moist-looking peaks, then gradually whisk in the hot syrup. The mixture will become shiny and start to thicken. Add the strawberry extract and whisk for 5–10 minutes, until the mixture is stiff enough to hold its shape on the whisk.

5. Spoon the mixture into the prepared baking tray and smooth using a wet palette knife. Sprinkle over the food colouring and use a small skewer to marble it through on the surface. Leave to set for 1 hour.

6. Loosen the marshmallow around the sides of the tray using a round-bladed knife, then turn it out onto a board. Cut it into 32 squares, then lightly dust with cornflour and sifted icing sugar. Place on a wire rack to dry. Serve immediately.

Apple and apricot fruit jellies

Makes: 30
Prep: 25 minutes
Cook: 10 minutes
Set: 3–4 hours

Called 'jujubes' in many countries, these fruity cubes are refreshing and delicious. You can change the fruit flavour simply by using a different fruit juice and jam.

450 ml/16 fl oz clear apple juice

3 tbsp powdered gelatine

400 g/14 oz caster sugar

500 g/1 lb 2 oz apricot jam

1. Put half the apple juice into a mixing bowl, then sprinkle the gelatine over the surface, making sure the powder is absorbed (see page 116). Set aside for 10 minutes.

2. Meanwhile, put the remaining apple juice and half the sugar into a heavy-based saucepan. Boil, stirring, for 5–6 minutes, or until the sugar has dissolved. Whisk in the jam, then return to the boil and cook for 3–4 minutes, until the mixture is thick and syrupy. Whisk the gelatine into the syrup until it dissolves.

3. Pour the mixture through a fine-mesh sieve into a bowl. Transfer it to a 25 x 17-cm/10 x 7-inch non-stick cake tin. Chill in the fridge for 3–4 hours, or until set.

4. Spread the remaining sugar over a large baking tray. Cut the fruit jelly into 30 squares and remove from the tin using a palette knife. Toss in the sugar to coat just before serving. Serve, or store in an airtight container in a cool, dry place for up to 5 days.

Raspberry coconut ice

Makes: 20
Prep: 30 minutes
Set: 3 hours

a little sunflower oil, for greasing

325 g/11½ oz icing sugar, sifted,
plus extra if needed

325 g/11½ oz sweetened
desiccated coconut

400 g/14 oz canned sweetened
full-fat condensed milk

1 tsp vanilla extract

55 g/2 oz raspberries

½ tsp pink food colouring

1 tsp raspberry extract

A no-cook sweet treat that is perfect to make with the kids. This is a lovely gift when wrapped in cellophane bags or little gift boxes.

1. Lightly brush a 20-cm/8-inch square baking tin with oil. Line the base with non-stick baking paper.

2. Put half the sifted icing sugar and half the coconut into one mixing bowl and put the other half into a second bowl. Stir the contents of each bowl, then make a well in the centre.

3. Add half the condensed milk and half the vanilla to each of the coconut mixtures and stir. Press one of the mixtures into the prepared tin and level using a spatula.

4. Put the raspberries into a blender and whizz to a purée. Push this through a sieve into a bowl to remove the seeds. Add the purée, food colouring and raspberry extract to the remaining coconut mixture. Add more sifted icing sugar if the mixture is too wet.

5. Spread the pink coconut ice over the white coconut layer, cover, then chill in the fridge for 3 hours, or until set.

6. Lift the coconut ice out of the tin, peel off the paper and cut into 20 squares. Store in an airtight container in a cool, dry place for up to 5 days.

Mini toffee apples

Makes: 12
Prep: 25 minutes
Cook: 20–25 minutes

Nothing beats the crunch of a homemade toffee apple on an autumnal evening. Pack these mini treats for an extra surprise at a Bonfire Night get-together.

3 large red apples

juice of 1 lemon

100 g/3½ oz caster sugar

175 ml/6 fl oz water

15 g/½ oz unsalted butter

a few drops of red food colouring

1. Put a bowl of iced water in the fridge. Using a melon scoop, scoop out 12 balls from the apples, making sure each ball has some red skin on it. Push a small skewer into each ball through the red skin. Squeeze over the lemon juice to prevent the apple from discolouring and set aside.

2. Put the sugar, water and butter into a medium heavy-based saucepan. Heat gently until the sugar has dissolved, tilting the pan to mix the ingredients together. Increase the heat and boil rapidly for 12–15 minutes, or until the mixture reaches 160°C/320°F on a sugar thermometer and is deep golden. Turn off the heat, stir in the food colouring and allow the bubbles to subside.

3. Remove the bowl of iced water from the fridge. Working as quickly as possible, dip the apples into the toffee one at a time, rotating them a few times to get an even coating, then drop them into the iced water for 30 seconds. Serve immediately.

Pistachio and apricot nougat

Makes: 16
Prep: 30 minutes
Cook: 15 minutes
Set: 8–10 hours

A confection made from boiled honey and sugar syrup mixed with beaten egg white, nuts and dried fruit. It is associated with the French town of Montélimar, where it has been made since the 18th century. Enjoy it as an after dinner sweet with coffee, crumble it over ice cream or use it in desserts and puddings.

edible rice paper

250 g/9 oz caster sugar

125 ml/4 fl oz liquid glucose

85 g/3 oz runny honey

2 tbsp water

a pinch of salt

1 egg white

½ tsp vanilla extract

60 g/2¼ oz unsalted butter, softened and diced

50 g/1¾ oz pistachio nuts, roughly chopped

50 g/1¾ oz ready-to-eat dried apricots, finely chopped

1. Line a 17-cm/7-inch square loose-bottomed cake tin with cling film, leaving an overhang. Line the base with edible rice paper.

2. Put the sugar, glucose, honey, water and salt into a heavy-based saucepan. Heat gently until the sugar has dissolved, tilting the pan to mix the ingredients together. Increase the heat and boil for 8 minutes, or until the mixture reaches 121°C/250°F on a sugar thermometer.

3. Put the egg white into an electric mixer or use a handheld whisk, and beat until firm. Gradually pour in a quarter of the hot syrup in a thin stream while still beating the egg. Continue beating for 5 minutes, until the mixture is stiff enough to hold its shape on the whisk.

4. Put the pan containing the remaining syrup over a gentle heat for 2 minutes, or until the mixture reaches 143°C/290°F on a sugar thermometer. Gradually pour the syrup over the egg mixture while beating.

5. Add the vanilla and butter and beat for a further 5 minutes. Add the pistachios and apricots and stir.

6. Pour the mixture into the tin and level using a palette knife. Cover with edible rice paper and chill in the fridge for 8–10 hours, or until fairly firm.

7. Lift the nougat out of the tin and cut into 16 squares. Serve or store in an airtight container in the fridge for up to 5 days.

peanut butter and chocolate candy balls

Makes: 36
Prep: 25 minutes
Cook: 5 minutes
Set: 4–6 hours

This recipe uses plain chocolate to coat the peanut candy balls, but if you prefer you can use milk or white chocolate, or a mixture of the three.

250 g/9 oz smooth peanut butter

55 g/2 oz unsalted butter

20 g/¼ oz rice pops

200 g/7 oz icing sugar

200 g/7 oz plain chocolate, roughly chopped

1. Line 2 baking trays with non-stick baking paper. Melt the peanut butter and butter together in a heavy-based saucepan.

2. Put the rice pops and icing sugar into a large mixing bowl. Pour in the melted butter mixture, then stir. When cool enough to handle, using the palms of your hands, roll the mixture into 2.5-cm/1-inch balls, then put them on the prepared baking trays and chill in the fridge for 3–4 hours, or until firm.

3. Put the chocolate in a heatproof bowl, set the bowl over a saucepan of gently simmering water and heat until melted.

4. Using a teaspoon, dip the balls into the chocolate one by one, making sure they are covered completely, then lift them out and return them to the baking trays. Chill in the fridge for 1–2 hours, or until set. Serve or store in an airtight container in the fridge for up to 5 days.

Sea-salted pecan candies

Makes: 12
Prep: 15 minutes
Cook: 10–15 minutes
Set: 10 minutes

55 g/2 oz pecan nuts

300 g/10½ oz caster sugar

175 ml/6 fl oz water

2 tsp sea salt

You can replace the pecan nuts with walnuts, whole peeled almonds or cashew nuts if you prefer.

1. Preheat the grill to medium.

2. Put the pecans in a baking tray and toast them under the grill for 3–4 minutes, or until golden, shaking them halfway through. Divide the nuts between the sections of a 12-section silicone mini muffin tray.

3. Put the sugar and water into a heavy-based saucepan. Heat gently until the sugar has dissolved, tilting the pan to mix the ingredients together, until the mixture reaches an even light brown colour. Continue cooking until it is a slightly deeper brown, watching it carefully so it doesn't burn. Scatter in the sea salt.

4. Transfer the mixture into a jug and quickly pour it into the sections of the mini muffin tray. Leave to cool for 10 minutes, until the sweets set and harden. Turn the candies out of the tray. Store in an airtight container in a cool, dry place for up to 5 days.

Toffee popcorn

Makes: 200 g/7 oz
Prep: 15 minutes
Cook: 5–10 minutes

25 g/1 oz unsalted butter

55 g/2 oz popping corn

TOFFEE COATING

40 g/1½ oz unsalted butter

55 g/2 oz soft dark brown sugar

2 tbsp golden syrup

This popcorn is fun to make as a treat for children's birthday parties. For adults, sprinkle on a little cayenne pepper to get a sweet and spicy kick.

1. Melt the butter in a large heavy-based saucepan. Sprinkle in the popping corn and swirl the pan to coat the corn evenly.

2. Cover the pan with a tight-fitting lid, reduce the heat to low and let the corn start popping. Shake the pan a couple of times to move the unpopped pieces to the bottom. As soon as the popping stops, take the pan off the heat and leave it to stand, covered.

3. For the toffee coating, melt the butter in a medium heavy-based saucepan. Add the sugar and syrup and cook over a high heat, stirring, for 1–2 minutes, or until the sugar has dissolved.

4. Pour the toffee coating over the popped corn, replace the lid on the pan and shake well. Allow to cool slightly, then serve immediately.

Honeycomb brittle

Makes: approx 20
Prep: 15 minutes
Cook: 10–15 minutes
Set: 5 minutes

Known as hokey-pokey in Australia, this light and crunchy brittle is perfect broken into bite-size pieces or crushed over ice cream.

a little sunflower oil, for greasing

175 g/6 oz caster sugar

100 g/3½ oz golden syrup

100 g/3½ oz unsalted butter, diced

2 tsp bicarbonate of soda

1. Lightly brush a 20-cm/8-inch square baking tin with oil.

2. Put the sugar, syrup and butter into a large heavy-based saucepan. Heat gently until the sugar has dissolved, tilting the pan to mix the ingredients together. Increase the heat and boil rapidly for 4–5 minutes, or until the mixture goes a light golden colour.

3. Add the bicarbonate of soda and stir for a few seconds; be careful as the mixture will expand and bubble.

4. Pour the mixture into the prepared tin. Leave to cool for 5 minutes, or until set. Break the brittle into shards. Store in an airtight container in a cool, dry place for up to 2 weeks.

Sesame, marshmallow and cranberry squares

Makes: 20

Prep: 15 minutes

Cook: 20 minutes

These are best baked in advance. They make a great teatime treat or lunchbox filler.

150 g/5½ oz medium oatmeal

55 g/2 oz sesame seeds

40 g/1½ oz light brown sugar

35 g/1¼ oz mini marshmallows

70 g/2½ oz dried cranberries

8 tbsp runny honey

5 tbsp sunflower oil, plus extra for greasing

a few drops of vanilla extract

1. Preheat the oven to 160°C /325°F/Gas Mark 3. Lightly brush a 28 x 18-cm/11 x 7-inch baking tin with oil. Line the base with non-stick baking paper.

2. Put the oatmeal, sesame seeds, sugar, marshmallows and cranberries into a mixing bowl and stir. Make a well in the centre, add the honey, oil and vanilla extract then stir again.

3. Press the mixture into the prepared tin and level using a metal spoon. Bake in the preheated oven for 20 minutes, or until golden and bubbling.

4. Leave to cool in the tin for 10 minutes, then cut into small squares. Leave to cool completely before turning out of the tin. Store in an airtight container in a cool, dry place for up to 2 days.

Cashew nut brittle

Makes: approx 20
Prep: 15 minutes
Cook: 25–30 minutes

150 g/5½ oz roasted, salted cashew nuts
....
350 g/12 oz caster sugar
....
¼ tsp cream of tartar
....
175 ml/6 fl oz water
....
15 g/½ oz unsalted butter
....

This is a wonderful, buttery brittle that is easy to make and wows everyone! You could use roasted peanuts instead of cashews, if you prefer.

1. Line a 20-cm/8-inch square baking tin with non-stick baking paper.

2. Spread the cashew nuts over the baking tin in a thin, even layer.

3. Put the sugar, cream of tartar and water into a heavy-based saucepan. Bring to a gentle boil over a medium heat, stirring all the time.

4. Reduce the heat to low and simmer for 20–25 minutes without stirring, until the mixture reaches 143°C/290°F on a sugar thermometer. Stir in the butter, then carefully drizzle the caramel over the nuts. Leave to cool completely.

5. Break the brittle into shards. Serve or store in an airtight container in a cool, dry place for up to 2 days.

Vanilla fudge

Makes: 16
Prep: 15 minutes
Cook: 10–15 minutes
Set: 1 hour

Just five simple ingredients and you can make the creamiest vanilla fudge ever. A guaranteed hit! Be careful when you stir the fudge, as the mixture is very hot.

a little sunflower oil, for greasing

450 g/1 lb caster sugar

85 g/3 oz unsalted butter

150 ml/5 fl oz full-fat milk

150 ml/5 fl oz evaporated milk

2 tsp vanilla extract

1. Lightly brush a 20-cm/8-inch square baking tin with oil. Line it with non-stick baking paper, snipping diagonally into the corners, then pressing the paper into the tin so that the base and sides are lined.

2. Put the sugar, butter, milk and evaporated milk into a heavy-based saucepan. Heat gently, stirring, until the sugar has dissolved.

3. Increase the heat and boil for 12–15 minutes, or until the mixture reaches 116°C/240°F on a sugar thermometer (if you don't have a sugar thermometer, spoon a little of the syrup into some iced water; it will form a soft ball when it is ready). As the temperature rises, stir the fudge occasionally so the sugar doesn't stick and burn.

4. Remove the pan from the heat, add the vanilla and beat using a wooden spoon until thickened.

5. Pour the mixture into the prepared tin and smooth the surface using a spatula. Leave to cool for 1 hour, or until set.

6. Lift the fudge out of the tin, peel off the paper and cut into small squares. Store in an airtight container in a cool, dry place for up to 2 weeks.

Indulgent whisky fudge

Makes: 16
Prep: 15 minutes
Cook: 10–15 minutes
Set 2–3 hours

If you are a chocolate and whisky lover, this is the perfect edible treat for you. You can use a good brandy instead of whisky, if you prefer.

a little sunflower oil, for greasing

250 g/9 oz soft brown sugar

100 g/3½ oz unsalted butter, diced

400 g/14 oz canned sweetened full-fat condensed milk

2 tbsp glucose syrup

25 g/1 oz walnut pieces

150 g/5½ oz plain chocolate, roughly chopped

60 ml/2¼ fl oz Scotch whisky

1. Lightly brush a 20-cm/8-inch square baking tin with oil. Line it with non-stick baking paper, snipping diagonally into the corners, then pressing the paper into the tin so that the base and sides are lined.

2. Put the sugar, butter, condensed milk and glucose into a heavy-based saucepan. Heat gently, stirring, until the sugar has dissolved.

3. Increase the heat and boil for 12–15 minutes, or until the mixture reaches 116°C/240°F on a sugar thermometer (if you don't have a sugar thermometer, spoon a little of the syrup into some iced water; it will form a soft ball when it is ready). As the temperature rises, stir the fudge occasionally so the sugar doesn't stick and burn. Remove the fudge from the heat. Add the chocolate and whisky and stir together until the chocolate has melted and the mixture is smooth.

4. Preheat the grill to medium–hot. Put the walnuts in a baking tray and toast them under the grill for 2–3 minutes, or until browned. Roughly chop them.

5. Pour the mixture into the prepared baking tin, smooth the surface using a spatula and sprinkle over the walnuts. Leave to cool for 1 hour. Cover with cling film, then chill in the fridge for 1–2 hours, or until firm. Lift the fudge out of the tin, peel off the paper and cut into small squares. Store in an airtight container in a cool, dry place for up to 2 weeks.

Chocolate pretzel fudge squares

Makes: 16
Prep: 15 minutes
Cook: 8–10 minutes
Set: 2–3 hours

These are so easy to make. The salty pretzels counteract the rich sweetness of the chocolate and condensed milk.

175 g/6 oz mini pretzels

a little sunflower oil, for greasing

2 tbsp unsalted butter, diced

300 g/10½ oz milk chocolate chips

400 g/14 oz canned sweetened full-fat condensed milk

1 tsp vanilla extract

1. Roughly chop 55 g/2 oz of the pretzels.

2. Lightly brush a 24-cm/10-inch square baking tin with oil. Line it with non-stick baking paper, snipping diagonally into the corners, then pressing the paper into the tin so that the base and sides are lined and there is a 5-cm/2-inch overhang on all sides.

3. Put the butter, chocolate chips, condensed milk and vanilla in a heatproof bowl, set the bowl over a saucepan of gently simmering water and heat, stirring occasionally, for 8–10 minutes, or until the chocolate has just melted and the mixture is smooth and warm but not hot. Remove from the heat and stir in the chopped pretzels.

4. Pour the mixture into the prepared tin, smooth the surface using a spatula and push in the whole pretzels. Leave to cool for 1 hour. Cover with cling film, then chill in the fridge for 1–2 hours, or until firm.

5. Lift the fudge out of the tin, peel off the paper and cut it into small squares. Store in an airtight container in a cool, dry place for up to 2 weeks.

Chocolate-coated candied orange rind

Makes: 36
Prep: 55 minutes
Cook: 1 hour
Set: 2-4 hours

Strips of candied orange rind dipped in plain chocolate make an elegant gift. Alternatively, serve them with coffee after dinner.

3 large navel oranges
....
200 g/7 oz granulated sugar
....
200 ml/7 fl oz water
....
200 g/7 oz plain chocolate,
roughly chopped
....

1. Using a sharp knife, cut the rind off the oranges, then remove the white pith from the rind. Slice the rind into 36 x 6 x 1-cm/2½ x ½-inch strips, discarding any you don't need.

2. Bring a small saucepan of water to the boil, then add the orange rind and simmer for 10 minutes. Drain, then rinse under cold running water. Pour more water into the pan and bring it to the boil again, then return the rind to the pan and simmer for a further 10 minutes. Repeat this process one more time.

3. Put the sugar and water into a heavy-based saucepan. Bring it to the boil and simmer gently, stirring, for 5 minutes, or until the sugar has dissolved and the mixture has reduced a little in volume. Add the orange rind and continue simmering for 15 minutes. Transfer the candied peel to a wire rack and leave to cool for 1-2 hours, or overnight. Line a baking tray with non-stick baking paper.

4. Put the chocolate in heatproof bowl, set the bowl over a saucepan of gently simmering water and heat until melted.

5. Dip a third of the length of each candied orange strip in the chocolate and place it on the prepared baking tray. Leave to cool for 1-2 hours, or until set. Store in an airtight container in a cool, dry place for up to 5 days.

Salted caramel and chocolate bites

Makes: 20
Prep: 30 minutes
Cook: 35–40 minutes

Sea salt and caramel is a classic combination, and here it is enhanced by the addition of walnuts.

a little sunflower oil, for greasing

200 g/7 oz plain chocolate, roughly chopped

150 g/5½ oz unsalted butter

2 eggs

175 g/6 oz soft light brown sugar

55 g/2 oz plain flour

1 tsp baking powder

55 g/2 oz walnut pieces, roughly chopped

6 tbsp caramel (dulce de leche)

1 tbsp sea salt

1. Preheat the oven to 170°C/325°F/Gas Mark 3. Lightly brush a 20-cm/8-inch square baking tin with oil. Line it with non-stick baking paper, snipping diagonally into the corners, then pressing the paper into the tin so that the base and sides are lined.

2. Put 70 g/2½ oz chocolate and all the butter in a heatproof bowl, set the bowl over a saucepan of gently simmering water and heat until melted, stirring from time to time.

3. Put the eggs and sugar into a mixing bowl, then sift in the flour and baking powder. Stir in the melted chocolate mixture and beat together until blended. Add the walnuts and remaining chocolate and stir together. Pour the mixture into the prepared tin and smooth the surface using a spatula.

4. Put the caramel into a small mixing bowl and beat, then swirl it through the chocolate mixture using a fork. Scatter over the sea salt and bake in the preheated oven for 30–35 minutes, or until the cake begins to shrink slightly from the sides of the tin. Leave to cool for 1 hour.

5. Lift the cake out of the tin, peel off the paper and cut it into small squares. Store in an airtight container in a cool, dry place for up to 2 days.

White and dark chocolate-dipped strawberries

Makes: 24
Prep: 10 minutes
Cook: 3–4 minutes
Set: 1 hour

Chocolate always makes a sweet special and, in this fun, party treat, it is paired with luscious strawberries. Prepare it several hours before you plan to serve it if you wish.

100 g/3½ oz plain chocolate, roughly chopped

100 g/3½ oz white chocolate, roughly chopped

24 large strawberries

1. Line a baking tray with non-stick baking paper. Put the plain chocolate and white chocolate into 2 separate heatproof bowls, set the bowls over 2 saucepans of gently simmering water and heat until melted.

2. Dip the pointed end of each strawberry into one of the melted chocolates and transfer it to the prepared baking tray. Leave to cool for 1 hour, or until set.

3. Put each strawberry in a liqueur glass or on a plate and serve immediately.

Mini cranberry and ginger florentines

Makes: 48
Prep: 30 minutes
Cook: 15–20 minutes
Set: 2 hours

These crispy and chewy bites are an Italian classic and make a marvellous present.

70 g/2½ oz muscovado sugar

55 g/2 oz runny honey

100 g/3½ oz unsalted butter, plus extra for greasing

50 g /1¾ oz desiccated coconut

70 g/2½ oz flaked almonds

1 tbsp finely chopped candied peel

1 tbsp finely chopped crystallized stem ginger

100 g/3½ oz dried cranberries

50 g/1¾ oz plain flour, plus extra for dusting

250 g/9 oz plain chocolate, roughly chopped

1. Preheat the oven to 180°C/350°F/Gas Mark 4. Lightly grease with butter 4 x 12-section mini muffin tins (the base of each cup should be 2 cm/¾ inch in diameter), then lightly dust them with flour.

2. Put the sugar, honey and butter into a heavy-based saucepan. Heat gently, stirring, until the sugar has dissolved, tilting the pan to mix the ingredients together. Stir in the coconut, almonds, candied peel, crystallized ginger, cranberries and flour.

3. Put small teaspoonfuls of the mixture into the prepared muffin tins. Bake in the preheated oven for 10–12 minutes, or until golden brown. Leave to cool in the tins for 1 hour. Using a palette knife, transfer to a wire rack to firm up.

4. Meanwhile, put the chocolate in a heatproof bowl, set the bowl over a saucepan of gently simmering water and heat until melted.

5. Dip each florentine into the melted chocolate so the base is covered. Place on a wire rack, chocolate side up, and leave to set for 1 hour. Store in an airtight container in a cool, dry place for up to 2 days.

nutty peppermint bark

Makes: approx 25
Prep: 20 minutes
Cook: 3–4 minutes
Set: 30 minutes

200 g/7 oz red and white striped peppermint candy canes, broken into pieces

500 g/1 lb 2 oz white chocolate, roughly chopped

100 g/3½ oz chopped mixed nuts

Kids and adults alike will love this treat. If you can't get hold of peppermint candy canes, substitute them with any mint candy.

1. Line a 30 x 20-cm/12 x 8-inch baking tin with non-stick baking paper.

2. Put the broken candy into a large plastic food bag and seal tightly. Using a rolling pin, bash the bag until the candy is crushed into small pieces.

3. Put the chocolate in a heatproof bowl, set the bowl over a saucepan of gently simmering water and heat until melted. Remove from the heat and stir in three quarters of the candy.

4. Pour the mixture into the prepared baking tin, smooth the surface using a spatula and sprinkle over the chopped nuts and remaining candy. Press down very slightly to ensure they stick. Cover with cling film and chill in the fridge for 30 minutes, or until firm.

5. Break the peppermint bark into small, uneven pieces. Store in an airtight container in a cool, dry place for up to 2 weeks.

Peppermint creams

Makes: 25
Prep: 30 minutes
Set: 25 hours

1 large egg white

325 g/11½ oz icing sugar, sifted, plus extra for dipping if needed

a few drops of peppermint extract

a few drops of green food colouring

100 g/3½ oz plain chocolate, roughly chopped

The pretty and tasty peppermint cream is an old-fashioned favourite. It's a refreshing choice for an after dinner sweet.

1. Line a baking tray with non-stick baking paper.

2. Lightly whisk the egg white in a large, clean mixing bowl until it is frothy but still translucent.

3. Add the sifted icing sugar to the egg white and stir using a wooden spoon until the mixture is stiff. Knead in the peppermint extract and food colouring.

4. Using the palms of your hands, roll the mixture into walnut-sized balls and place them on the prepared baking tray. Use a fork to flatten them; if it sticks to them, dip it in icing sugar before pressing. Put the creams in the fridge to set for 24 hours.

5. Put the chocolate in a heatproof bowl, set the bowl over a saucepan of gently simmering water and heat until melted. Dip the creams halfway in the chocolate and return to the baking tray for 1 hour, or until set. Store in an airtight container in the fridge for up to 5 days.

Plain chocolate and amaretto truffles

Makes: 12
Prep: 30 minutes
Soak: 6–8 hours
Cook: 5–10 minutes
Set: 1–2 hours

These delectable morsels are so easy to make and look really glamorous! Use any liqueur instead of the amaretto if you wish.

50 ml/2 fl oz amaretto liqueur

55 g/2 oz sultanas

100 g/3½ oz plain chocolate, roughly chopped

2 tbsp double cream

70 g/2½ oz ready-made chocolate cake or brownie, crumbled

100 g/3½ oz hazelnuts

55 g/2 oz chocolate sprinkles, to decorate

1. Put the amaretto and sultanas into a small mixing bowl, cover and leave to soak for 6–8 hours. Line a baking tray with non-stick baking paper.

2. Transfer the amaretto mixture to a food processor and whizz until puréed.

3. Put the chocolate and cream in a heatproof bowl, set the bowl over a saucepan of gently simmering water and heat until melted. Remove from the heat, add the amaretto purée and chocolate cake and stir well.

4. When cool enough to handle, using the palms of your hands, roll the mixture into truffle-sized balls and place on the prepared baking tray.

5. Preheat the grill to medium. Put the hazelnuts on a second baking tray and toast them under the grill for 2–3 minutes, or until browned, shaking them halfway through. Finely chop them.

6. Spread the chocolate sprinkles onto one plate and the hazelnuts onto another. Roll half the truffles in the chocolate and half in the hazelnuts. Return to the baking tray, cover with non-stick baking paper and chill in the fridge for 1–2 hours, or until firm. Store in an airtight container in the fridge for up to 5 days.

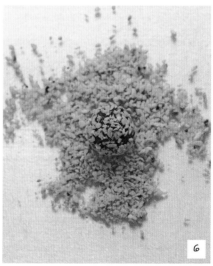

Lemon and white chocolate creams

Makes: 12
Prep: 40 minutes
Cook: 5–10 minutes
Set: 13–18 hours

For an Oriental twist on these decadent truffles, add a large pinch of ground cardamom seeds and star anise to the cream and chocolate mixture.

300 g/10½ oz white chocolate, roughly chopped

2 tbsp double cream

finely grated rind of 1 lemon

2 tbsp limoncello

55 g/2 oz unsalted butter, softened and diced

25 g/1 oz pistachio nuts, finely chopped

1. Put 100 g/3½ oz chocolate and all the cream in a heatproof bowl, set the bowl over a saucepan of gently simmering water and heat until melted.

2. Remove from the heat, add the lemon rind, limoncello and butter and whisk for 3–4 minutes, or until thickened. Transfer to an airtight container and chill in the fridge for 6–8 hours, or until firm.

3. Line a baking tray with non-stick baking paper. Scoop teaspoonfuls of the mixture and, using the palms of your hands, roll them into truffle-sized balls. Place the balls on the prepared tray, cover with cling film and freeze for 6–8 hours.

4. Put the remaining chocolate in a heatproof bowl, set the bowl over a saucepan of gently simmering water and heat until melted. Using 2 forks, dip each truffle into the chocolate to coat evenly. Return them to the prepared baking tray, sprinkle over the pistachios and chill in the fridge for 1–2 hours, or until firm. Store in an airtight container in the fridge for up to 5 days.

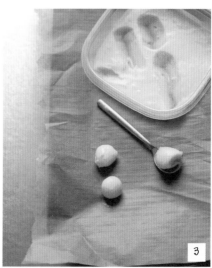

Espresso truffles

Makes: 12
Prep: 40 minutes
Cook: 5–10 minutes
Set: 13–18 hours

For a twist on these coffee truffles, simply replace the coffee liqueur with Irish cream liqueur or any orange-flavoured liqueur.

300 g/10½ oz plain chocolate, roughly chopped

2 tbsp double cream

1 tbsp strong espresso coffee, cooled

2 tbsp coffee liqueur

55 g/2 oz unsalted butter, softened and diced

edible gold leaf, to decorate (optional)

1. Put 100 g/3½ oz chocolate and all the cream in a heatproof bowl, set the bowl over a saucepan of gently simmering water and heat until melted.

2. Remove from the heat, add the espresso, coffee liqueur and butter and whisk for 3–4 minutes, or until thickened. Transfer to an airtight container and chill in the fridge for 6–8 hours, or until firm.

3. Line a baking tray with non-stick baking paper. Scoop teaspoonfuls of the mixture and, using the palms of your hands, roll them into truffle-sized balls. Place the balls on the prepared tray, cover with cling film and freeze for 6–8 hours.

4. Put the remaining chocolate in a heatproof bowl, set the bowl over a saucepan of gently simmering water and heat until melted. Using 2 forks, dip each truffle into the chocolate to coat evenly. Return them to the prepared baking tray and chill in the fridge for 1–2 hours, or until firm. Top each truffle with edible gold paper to decorate, if desired. Store in an airtight container in the fridge for up to 5 days.

Chilli and cardamom chocolate thins

Makes: 40
Prep: 30 minutes
Cook: 5–10 minutes
Set: 1–2 hours

These simple treats are perfect for kids to make. They're ideal for putting into a pretty box and giving as a present too.

CHILLI PLAIN CHOCOLATE THINS

200 g/7 oz plain chocolate, roughly chopped

a large pinch of hot chilli powder

edible glitter, to decorate

CARDAMOM WHITE CHOCOLATE THINS

200 g/7 oz white chocolate, roughly chopped

½ tsp cardamom seeds, crushed

25 g/1 oz pistachio nuts, finely chopped, plus extra to decorate

edible glitter, to decorate

1. Line 4 baking trays with non-stick baking paper.

2. For the chilli plain chocolate thins, put the plain chocolate in a heatproof bowl, set the bowl over a saucepan of gently simmering water and heat until melted. Remove from the heat and stir in the chilli powder.

3. Drop teaspoonfuls of the chocolate mixture onto 2 of the prepared baking trays. Scatter over a little edible glitter before the chocolate sets. Leave to set in a cool place, but not in the fridge, for 1–2 hours.

4. For the cardamom white chocolate thins, put the white chocolate in a heatproof bowl, set the bowl over a saucepan of gently simmering water and heat until melted. Remove from the heat and stir in the cardamom and pistachios.

5. Drop teaspoonfuls of the white chocolate mixture onto the remaining 2 prepared baking trays. Scatter over the remaining chopped pistachios and a little edible glitter before the chocolate sets. Leave to set in a cool place, but not in the fridge, for 1–2 hours. Store in an airtight container in a cool, dry place for up to 5 days.

Iced citrus marzipan thins

Makes: 30
Prep: 25 minutes
Set: overnight

200 g/7 oz ground almonds

200 g/7 oz caster sugar

1 large egg

a few drops of citrus extract

finely grated rind of ½ orange

FOR THE ICING

200 g/7 oz fondant icing sugar,
sifted, plus extra for dusting

juice of 1 lemon

Originally from Aix-en-Provence in France, these easy-to-make after dinner treats are full of citrus and almond goodness.

1. Line a 20-cm/8-inch square baking tin with non-stick baking paper, snipping diagonally into the corners, then pressing the paper into the tin so that the base and sides are lined. Lightly dust a work surface with icing sugar.

2. Put the almonds and caster sugar into a mixing bowl and stir. Add the egg, citrus extract and orange rind and mix, using your hands, to form a stiff paste.

3. Knead the marzipan briefly on the prepared work surface, then press it into the base of the prepared tin using the back of a spoon, until even and smooth. Leave to set for 1 hour.

4. For the icing, put the sifted fondant icing sugar and lemon juice into a mixing bowl and stir until smooth, then spread evenly over the marzipan. Cover and leave in a cool place, but not the fridge, to dry overnight.

5. Cut the iced marzipan into bite-sized shapes of your choice using a fondant or cookie cutter. Store in an airtight container in the fridge for up to 2 days.

Index